# Stretch Yourself

## A Personalized Journey to Deepen Your Teaching Practice

CAITLIN McLEMORE
AND FANNY PASSEPORT

**International Society for Technology in Education**
PORTLAND, OREGON • ARLINGTON, VIRGINIA

## Dedication

*This book is dedicated to all the learners who live and breathe collaboration, and who want to accelerate change by generously giving back to the community.*

*Stretch Yourself*
*A Personalized Journey to Deepen Your Teaching Practice*
Caitlin McLemore and Fanny Passeport

© 2018 International Society for Technology in Education
World rights reserved. No part of this book may be reproduced or transmitted in any form or by any means—electronic, mechanical, photocopied, recorded, or by any information storage or retrieval system—without prior written permission from the publisher. Contact Permissions Editor: https://www.iste.org/resources/permissions-and-reprints; permissions@iste.org; (fax) 1.541.302.3780.

Project Editors: *Emily Reed and Valerie Witte*
Developmental Editor: *Lynda Gansel*
Copy Editor: *Jen Weaver-Neist*
Proofreader: *Kate Burke Bradley*
Indexer: *Valerie Haynes Perry*
Book Design and Production: *Mayfly Design*
Cover Design: *Eddie Oullette*

Library of Congress Cataloging-in-Publication Data available

First Edition
ISBN: 978-1-56484-748-5
Ebook version available

Printed in the United States of America
ISTE® is a registered trademark of the International Society for Technology in Education.

# About ISTE

The International Society for Technology in Education (ISTE) is the premier nonprofit organization serving educators and education leaders committed to empowering connected learners in a connected world. ISTE serves more than 100,000 education stakeholders throughout the world.

ISTE's innovative offerings include the ISTE Conference & Expo—one of the biggest, most comprehensive edtech events in the world—as well as the widely adopted ISTE Standards for learning, teaching, and leading in the digital age; and a robust suite of professional learning resources, including webinars, online courses, consulting services for schools and districts, books, and peer-reviewed journals and publications. Visit ISTE.org to learn more.

## Related ISTE Titles

*Sketchnoting in the Classroom: A Practical Guide to Deepen Student Learning*

By Nichole Carter

*Pathways to Well-being: Helping Educators (and Others) Find Balance in a Connected World*

By Susan Brooks-Young and Sara Armstrong

To see all books available from ISTE, please visit https://www.iste.org/resources.

# From the Authors

Credit: Joe Croker

I am currently the academic technology specialist at Harpeth Hall School, an independent college-preparatory school for young women in Grades 5–12 located in Nashville, Tennessee. In my role, I work with faculty and students to foster effective and meaningful technology integration within the classroom curriculum. I also facilitate and lead design and innovation projects in our school makerspace. In 2018, our middle school program was proud to be named a finalist for the Future of Education Technology Conference STEM Excellence Award.

Also in 2018, I received the Outstanding Young Educator Award by ISTE, and I was named an Emerging Leader by ISTE in 2017. I was also part of the winning team for the ISTE Librarians Network Technology Innovation Primary Award in 2014.

My career in education has been—and continues to be—a great reward. I am honored to have ongoing opportunities to serve the education community. My volunteer work for ISTE is particularly important to me, and I have contributed in a variety of roles, such as an annual conference proposal review chair, award judge, beta tester for Verizon Mobile Learning Academy (VMLA), Board Ballot Selection Committee member, Student Standards Refresh Committee member, and Young Educator Network (YEN) scholarship mentor. Additionally, I was on the YEN leadership team from 2017–18. Before YEN, I served on the leadership team of the Mobile Learning Network from 2013–17, including service as president and communications chair.

In 2010, I earned a master of education (M.Ed.) degree in elementary education, with a specialization in educational technology, from the University of Florida. I am currently a doctoral candidate at Johns Hopkins University pursuing a doctor of education (Ed.D.) degree, with a specialization in technology integration in K–16 education. My research focuses on preparing middle school students for successful participation in the digital age through development of critical information literacy skills.

Fun fact: In 2014, I read all 90+ Newbery Award–winning books, in order, and blogged about them at readnewberys.blogspot.com. (I have also read the winner each year since.)

Happy reading!

—Caitlin McLemore
(On Twitter @edtechcaitlin)

 I have been working as an educational technology coach at Mercedes-Benz International School (PK–12) in Pune, India, for the past three years. I graduated with a master's degree in ethnoecology (a mix of ethnology and ecology) in 2009 and carried out my fieldwork in the Indian Himalayas. While studying ethnoecology, I enrolled in an online course on French foreign language teaching pedagogy. Upon completion, I started teaching English as a second language in France and then moved to India to teach French in international schools.

The more I used Moodle as part of my teaching practice, the more my interest in blended learning grew. I became a tech-savvy colleague, helping others with technical glitches as I read more about technology integration. It was only when I became a Google-certified teacher (in 2014) that I really entered the edtech sphere. I collected edtech badges and certificates, as these titles helped me get recognized and feel valued. They also opened up multiple networks of like-minded people with whom I often collaborate. From a tool-centered approach, I slowly developed an understanding of the impact and purpose of edtech, which I share on my website and blog, No BordersLearning.com.

I am heavily involved with ISTE, having volunteered in the leadership of the Young Educator Network (YEN). As a result of this work, I was awarded the 2016 ISTE Edtech Coach PLN Award, one of the 2016 Emerging Leader awards, and the 2017 Outstanding Young Educator Award.

Something special: I teach French as a foreign language using the Silent Way, which is a pedagogical approach created by Caleb Gattegno. This means that I don't provide a model to repeat and can teach without speaking much!

I hope you enjoy the process of reading this book and making the ideas yours.

—Fanny Passeport
(On Twitter @fanny_passeport)

 Both of us are edtech coaches who enjoy actively engaging with ISTE as volunteer leaders of the YEN professional learning community, which is now an input group. Throughout our time with ISTE, we have enjoyed collaborating, listening, sharing, and learning from other ISTE members. In particular, we have always been interested in backward design and pedagogy. One of our main interests in writing *Stretch Yourself* was to place emphasis on the learning rather than the technology. In the process, we realized our key concept was flexibility. When we stretch ourselves as individuals *and* as educators, we discover new qualities within ourselves. We find the power to consider new alternatives, take risks, and share with other educators as we continue our learning journey. We build muscles that we didn't even know existed!

We met through ISTE in June 2017 and have been collaborating very closely since then. As we developed a strong partnership and shared our thirst for learning with each other, we decided to share our ideas and passions with a wider audience by cowriting this book. We were especially interested in sharing our own experiences when we started with technology integration, recalling our fears and excitements, our hopes and failures, and our needs and wants. We wanted to share some of our best resources while also modeling personalized learning. Therefore, we made it our goal to produce a book that could be consumed as well as cocreated.

*Stretch Yourself* is for educators starting in the profession or those looking for a way to reflect on her or his digital-age practices. Beyond serving the needs of young or new educators, we think that anyone interested in growing can benefit from reading this book and engaging in the process that we created.

We hope that you enjoy our book. Read, think, write, and make it your own. Happy reading and good luck on your stretching journey!

—Caitlin McLemore and Fanny Passeport

## Acknowledgments

**From Fanny:**

First of all, I am grateful to Caitlin for agreeing to coauthor this book with me and for bringing her insights, practice, and design-thinking mindset to the endeavor. Our collaboration has been smooth and enjoyable, and we will continue to stretch together!

I would like to thank my dear colleagues from "Subtle" (**Sub**ordination of Teaching **t**o **L**earning), in particular, Roslyn Young, who helped me refine my pedagogical approach in many ways in my first years of teaching. Unfortunately, our mutual friend and colleague, Glenys Hanson, passed away this year. I felt her presence throughout the writing of this book, as I have a special connection to her: she introduced me to the world of edtech. Thanks to her, my passion for technology continues to grow exponentially. I could never have come this far without her in my life; she inspired me, and I miss her dearly.

I would also like to acknowledge my mentors Eileen Niedermann, Helen Sharrock, and Daisy Rana for their trust and drive: Eileen for all the generative conversations we have every Thursday morning at 7:30! Helen for pushing me to continuously improve my practice. And Daisy for our peer-coaching sessions at school.

Thank you to Professor Oddball for the help in brainstorming some of this book's exercises and for the atmospheric music of the mindfulness meditation.

Thank you to my friend Maryln D'Souza for inspiring me with her drive, to my neighbors Gita and Jan who helped me test the quiz and improve it and fed me when I was busy writing so I would not have to spend time cooking for myself!

Lastly, thank you to the real everyday heroes: the students and teachers I work with. They bring me in contact with myself and provide me with many opportunities to grow and refine my craft. I am forever grateful for that.

**From Caitlin:**

There are so many people who contributed to this book in one way or another. However, a few specific acknowledgments are needed. Thank you to …

Fanny for inviting me to collaborate on this book. I value our friendship and look forward to continued collaboration.

The students at Harpeth Hall for being outstanding girls and young women. You inspire me to strive for excellence. Also, the faculty at Harpeth Hall for being eager and willing collaborators in the quest for innovation. In particular, Molly Rumsey for supporting all of my professional projects, both in and out of school. Your support gives me the space to stretch myself as an educator.

Lisa Sjogren and Nancye Blair Black for your mentorship and support as colleagues. You both helped me to get involved in YEN, which has been a meaningful and productive experience.

Kevin Goscha for trusting me in my first years as a tech integrationist and encouraging me to join ISTE on my very first day on the job. Your mentorship, early on, helped me to become the educator that I am today.

The professors at Johns Hopkins University School of Education and the University of Florida College of Education for providing me with the necessary knowledge and tools to be a confident and successful edtech educator. In particular, thank you to Dr. Wendy Drexler for being an ISTE guru and my dissertation advisor.

A special thank you to Kyle McLemore for constantly encouraging me in my stretching journey. You are always eager to help me achieve my dreams and goals, and for that, I am forever grateful.

Fanny and I also have some joint acknowledgements that we would like to make. Thank you to …

Richard Culatta, ISTE CEO, for valuing the voice of the young educators as a critical constituency within ISTE.

Our acquisitions editor, Valerie Witte, for taking on our project and working with us to make it a great product. Our managing editor, Emily Reed, for taking our words and making us sound even better. Our designer, Ryan Scheife, for making such great graphics and illustrations for the book! Thank you also to all the other editors and ISTE staff members who worked to make this book great.

Simon Helton, Heidi Ellis, and Lauren Kocher, who are our ISTE community rock stars! We work closely with them and appreciate their willingness to support us in everything we do. They are always open to hearing new ideas, eager to facilitate meaningful edtech integration, and available to connect educators within and beyond ISTE.

# Contents

## PART 1: Breathe

## PART 2: Stretch

## PART 3: Meditate

# Introduction

"The mind is just like a muscle—the more you exercise it,
the stronger it gets and the more it can expand."

—Idowu Koyenikan, *Wealth for All: Living a Life of Success
at the Edge of Your Ability*

You are someone who embraces challenge, desires innovation, and looks for ways to expand your personal capacity. We understand your drive to improve and stretch yourself; that is why we wrote this book. This book will help you to develop as a conscious, learning-centered, reflective, and collaborative educator. While we incorporate educational technology as a critical component of the classroom learning experience, the focus is on pedagogical best practices and on doing what is right for your students and for your professional growth too. We know you are up for the challenge, and we hope this book will support you on your stretching journey.

We designed this book to be an active and personalized learning journey to help you innovate in your classroom. You will explore your educational values and beliefs, engage in activities that will extend your capacities, and analyze your own learning processes. Not only will the book include text for you to read and reflect upon, but it will also include activities, exercises, recommended resources, and tools to use along the way.

Through reading this book and adding your own reflections, you will learn or continue learning how to use educational technology in meaningful ways, deepening your teaching practice. We will dive into the importance and purpose of edtech as well as discuss how to keep a pedagogical focus as you read and implement ideas. Rather than a focus on technology tools, the learning goals and pedagogy should be a priority, along with your educational values and beliefs, such as your school's vision and mission. You will learn to make the tools less and less visible as the technology becomes integrated and effective throughout your classroom and teaching practices.

## Introducing Edtech Yoga

Why yoga? We chose yoga as the framework for this journey because it is something that we practice in our personal lives. Yoga provides a holistic way of advancing your learning practice, as it encompasses both the physical and the mental aspects of life. You may be a practicing yogi or you may not have any experience with yoga before reading this book, or perhaps you are somewhere in between. Regardless of your personal experience with yoga, you will be able to find meaning and value here. We felt that many of the yoga principles and concepts were easily relatable to all readers. Also, we practice yoga in our own lives to maintain physical well-being, to center ourselves, to stay calm, and to be present!

Yoga comes in many forms but all incorporate the ideas of breath, poses and movements, and meditation. The breath is a vital force that grounds you and brings you to the present moment. Breath is necessary for life, and as such, it is an essential element of yoga. Breath connects us with our activities, our environment, and our senses—some of the key goals of the physical practice of yoga as well. A physical yoga practice involves learning and trying to execute various poses that emphasize different physical strengths or parts of the body. And the physical practice is never complete; there is no finish line. Rather, each pose acts as a personal journey toward improvement. Some days, you might be able to pop up into a headstand without any difficulty, and some days, your legs might not make it off the ground. The goal is to continue working on yourself by focusing on the practice and on the connection with the breath. To further this, yoga uses meditation as a tool to focus the mind. Meditation involves observing your thoughts and being aware of the conscious and unconscious mind. It might involve a centering mantra, or it might just be observational. Either way, the goal of meditation is not to quiet the mind but to be present, open, and aware.

We've taken some of the concepts of yoga and turned them into edtech yoga. With the breath, we want to focus on elevating your consciousness and taking a good look at your current edtech teaching and learning practice. Taking a breath in edtech yoga allows you to assess where you are now so that you can better determine your goals for the future. With the physical practice of edtech yoga, we focus on the stretching aspects of the physical practice of yoga, which is needed in many of the poses. Stretching in edtech yoga is action oriented, teaching you what tools, or props, you might need to help you stretch and then guiding you in the development of an action plan for implementation. Finally, the meditative piece of edtech yoga is about the collaborative and reflective processes that help us grow as educators. Meditation in edtech yoga centers you as a connected and empowered edtech educator. As you concentrate on your purpose, your goal will slowly become visible; and you will start becoming self-reflective, self-compassionate, and more flexible.

## How Our Process Can Help You

In *Stretch Yourself*, you get to be both reader and writer! This book is not just written for you to passively read and consume; though you will have the traditional opportunity to read, you will also have the chance to contribute and personalize the content so that it's meaningful to your context. Do you remember reading interactive fiction books, such as the Choose Your Own Adventure series, in which the story unfolds based on your choices? Well, in a similar manner, our intent is to provide a book that you can personalize—one that is learner centered, self-paced, and will lead you to discover yourself and become your own hero! And the personalized learning in this book provides a process as well as activities that you can transfer to the classroom, with your students, wherever you teach around the world.

Our goal in writing *Stretch Yourself* was to deliver a message of empowerment to the reader. We did not say anything new in this book; rather, we tried to collate ideas that inspired us and that might also spark your curiosity and support your growth. We want to share our perspective on how to stretch yourself as an edtech educator just like we have—and continue to do—ourselves. The book is designed to be an active and unique experience for each individual reader.

As connected learners, we also wanted to integrate other educators' voices, so we asked individuals from our networks to share their own stretching stories and realizations. To honor their contributions and embed a diversity of voices, you will find their sayings throughout the book.

Most of the concepts discussed revolve around innovation and learning, with technology in the background. As we wrote the book, we learned, unlearned, and relearned what we thought we knew about education and educational technology. In writing, we experienced the same stretching journey that we hope you will experience as a reader.

Every one of you has the power to make a positive difference in the world of education, so whatever gems you find in yourself by reading and contributing your ideas in this book, share away by connecting with us on this website: noborderslearning.com/stretch-yourself

Your voice matters, and sharing will multiply your impact as you inspire others. We want you to take an active part in an interconnected world of changemakers.

## Book Organization

This book is divided into three parts—"Breathe," "Stretch," and "Meditate"—and each part connects to specific ISTE Standards for Educators:

**Part 1, "Breathe,"** is all about pausing, taking a step back, and elevating your consciousness about your potential as an innovative educator, igniting or reigniting your passion for education. It takes you through steps to live and adopt a growth mindset. It asks you to examine your dreams, aspirations, values, and beliefs; and it strives to acknowledge the hardship every educator might face, reminding you that you are not alone! This section is meant to be hopeful and action centric, providing practical and encouraging ways to put your vision into action or to reassess your actions, keeping your spirits up in the process. We want to move you from feeling isolated in your classroom to finding the courage to become a connected educator who cocreates diamond-shaped networks.

At the end of this part of the book, you should be aware of something that might have been dormant in you—something precious and exciting. While this will be rejuvenating and motivating, you may find yourself with more questions than answers! But rest assured: as you concentrate on your purpose, your goal *will* become visible and you *will* become self-reflective, self-compassionate, and increasingly flexible. You will also declutter your teaching and take meaningful action to empower yourself, gaining the confidence to be your emerging self!

**Part 2, "Stretch,"** starts by introducing technology *inside* a box in order to think about what might exist *outside* the box. That way, we can apply our creativity and critical thinking when designing learning engagements.

When we think technology, we often think about tools, sites, the internet, and tech gadgets and gizmos. However, *Stretch Yourself* would like to bring in less tech and more learning. This part of the book tackles the importance of curating as well as sharing ideas. It also brings you back to your situation, your field, and how you might need to put your vision into action, regardless of the challenges that you face and how you will inspire others when you share your experience. It deals with adopting an interactive mindset, designing safe and responsible technology use, and facilitating authentic student agency. It also helps you to keep your balance and cautions you to resist the urge to overstretch.

**Part 3, "Meditate,"** is all about reflecting and collaborating. It is meant to trigger introspection and deep thinking, and also support you when giving or receiving meaningful feedback. This section focuses on giving feedback in a coaching situation that actually helps individuals grow.

Reflectivity is an essential quality for educators because we live in a world that is ever changing—a point made more evident in the digital age. This part of the book reviews the tenets of true collaboration and encourages you to share your journey with others beyond the limits of your school, extending your learning while strengthening your identity as an empowered educator.

You will also notice the use of some tentative language throughout the book (the use of "might" dominates the use of "could" or "should," for example). This is intentional, as we thrive to embrace a design thinking approach. We want to let you be in charge and think deeply about yourself rather than disrupt your thinking by providing directives.

## How to Use This Book

Each chapter in the book will take you through a personalized learning process, with "Stretching Exercises"; supportive resources and tools ("Edtech Props," similar to yoga props, such as slings, straps, and blocks); self-reflection "Meditation Prompts"; and practical "Take a Breath" ideas to encourage input in your learning experience. This introduction as well as the chapters end with "Inspiration" sections featuring our book recommendations for further exploration.

It's not necessary to work linearly through the book. You may want to skip exercises and come back to them later. Or you may want to do the exercises now and then come back to do them again next year, to refresh your practice. No matter what, always start with the flexibility quiz (found later in this section) to assess your current practice and inclination to a certain profile or profiles. Each detailed profile description (appendix A) gives suggested chapters to focus your studies. From there, you can work through the other chapters and exercises as you are ready. Just don't try to do it all at once. Instead, refer back to certain components as they relate to the challenges you encounter in your everyday teaching practices.

The creative exercises and journaling spaces represent what Daniel Pink (2018) calls *midpoints*: times that can either generate sparks or slumps. To make the sparks fly, follow Pink's advice:

✦ Acknowledge midpoints; don't ignore them. The creative spaces in this book are here to help you pause and think about where you are. Avoid skipping them, as they provide opportunities for deep reflection, contributing immensely to your growth. Be principled and engage in those exercises to get the most out of this book.

✦ Use those midpoints to put your full attention on your new learning. Even if they aren't pleasant discoveries and they make you anxious, resist the urge to stress out and exert control over yourself. Welcome these moments and immerse yourself mindfully into them. As you do this, you will feel a sense of achievement and satisfaction that naturally dissolves your trepidation.

✦ Imagine that you are a little bit late. It's useful to feel (or pretend to feel) just a bit behind, as this motivates you to take action and accelerates your thinking process by honing in on the most important points. It's like tricking your brain into focusing.

We invite you to use the creative and interactive components in this book to make it your own. Through reading, you might find comfort and reassurance; and through journaling, you might find revelation and audacity. As an empowered learner, the opportunities to record your thinking and observations through a step-by-step process will help you design *your* growth and own it. In order to kick off this personalized journey to deepen your teaching practice, we have designed the following flexibility quiz to get you going in a fun and engaging way.

We want your reading of the book to be a journey of being present with yourself but also the impetus pushing you forward, stretching you as an educator and making a difference in your classroom. Being present is a simple concept but one that can be difficult to obtain. Being present means being aware of what is happening *here* and *now*. It means not worrying about what happened in the past or about what is to come; all that matters is the current task at hand. The concept of presence is similar to being attentive but does not carry the meaning of "paying attention," because you are completely and naturally focused, with no need to force yourself to concentrate.

# *Flexibility Quiz*

## An Exercise to Discover How Flexible You Are in Your Practice

You are going on a quest to find your inner strengths. In this quiz, be ready to reveal some of your preconceived notions or personal thoughts about your level of flexibility as an educator. Answer the questions honestly—trust your gut! And don't worry about cramming for it; this quiz is not about testing your content knowledge. While it will provide you with a score for each profile type, the goal is not to achieve a certain number. The score just acts as a guideline to reveal your inclination toward a personality profile, so that you can be more deliberate when reading this book.

After you complete the quiz, calculate your score in appendix A and then read more in-depth information, which also highlights those chapters you might pay closer attention to as you personalize your learning experience.

Ready? Here we go!

Choose only one answer per question. Circle your answer with a pencil or keep track of your answers in a separate location, like a journal.

1. If you had to choose a visual that represents your pedagogical beliefs, what would it look like?

   ♦ A photo of a passionate adventurer climbing a mountain
   ♥ A messy canvas
   ♠ A poster about a contest or competition
   ♦ A graph showing that effort is everything
   ♣ A collage of apps and edtech tools
   ⬤ A map showing people who are connected through networks

2. What might the perfect classroom look like?

   ♣ Students are silent, listening, and following your instructions.
   ♥ Students are hyperactive—it's loud and messy.

♠ Students take over, which means you might not reach your objective, but it's all about their voice anyway.

♦ Students are engaged and responsive. They feel in charge and are growing.

3.  When you think about "technology," you think about:

♥ PowerPoint (you like to have your slides ready and you reuse them every year)

♣ disappointments (whenever you try using technology, it fails!),

♠ apps and other tech tools (the more the tech, the happier you are!),

♦ the tinkering mindset (it's about troubleshooting, creativity, and critical thinking),

♣ old-school hardware (paper, pens, and blackboard), or

♥ Smart Boards (a more advanced way for you to show content to students than using a regular whiteboard).

4.  At the end of the week, you often feel:

♦ satisfied about your accomplishments and in control of the upcoming week;

♣ exhausted and ready for a break (planning for next week will have to wait!);

♠ ready to plan all your lessons for next week right away (you've got lots of research to do!);

♥ relieved that your improvisation succeeded this week and will likely succeed next week as well (TGIF!); or

♣ confident, because you just have to give your students the same reliable worksheets that you did last year.

5.  When asking a colleague for feedback, you are looking for:

♥ empathy and support,

♣ compliments and praise,

♠ ruthless and straightforward honesty,

♦ sincere suggestions to improve, or

♥ company—a chance to socialize!

6. When you have a conflict with colleagues, your usual solution is to:

   ♣ just drop it (you have other things to do!);
   ♠ fight to win the battle;
   (♦) be quietly frustrated and grumble in your corner, until it passes;
   ♥ take a moment to breathe, calm yourself, and engage in a dialogue to resolve the issue; or
   ♥ find all available evidence to prove you are right.

7. A colleague is upset and acting rude. You think this colleague:

   ♦ must be stressed out (you feel the need to empathise rather than judge);
   ♣ is always like this (seriously—you don't really care);
   ♠ can't be ignored (you harass the person until they tell you what's wrong);
   ♦ might need to talk (you email the person to offer a sympathetic ear if needed); or
   (♥) is someone interesting to gossip about with colleagues (you start delightfully chitchatting about him or her).

8. You are being observed in class as part of your appraisal. How do you feel during the evaluation?

   ♣ Scrutinized and criticized every step of the way
   ♦ Glad to show how your students are doing (You are in your element!)
   ♥ Surprised (You forgot it was today, but no big deal. You will improvise on the fly and should pass.)
   (♣) Stressed, exposed, and convinced that your students will take this as an opportunity to retaliate for some bad lessons in the past
   ♠ Confident (You are sure that you are going to pull this off and impress the evaluator. You aim to be recognized as the best teacher in the department!)

9. How often do you reflect on the best ways for you to grow professionally and become increasingly effective as a teacher?

♣ Hardly ever—it's a waste of time. You would rather finish your photocopying.

♦ Reflection is like breathing for you: it's an everyday part of who you are.

♥ You only think about it when you are formally asked to (at the end of a unit, at reporting time, etc.).

♥ Actually, never—you think of doing it but keep pushing it down in priority on your to-do list.

♠ You only consider it when you're facing competition and need to showcase your best work to impress others.

10. What is most important to you in student development: fostering students who:

♥ make the world a better place even if they don't ever learn any curriculum-specific content;

♣ score the best grades;

♦ think for themselves and are independent;

♠ become the next world leaders; or

♦ follow their passions and dreams?

11. When do you feel the most successful?

♠ When you exceed expectations and wow the people around you

♦ When you see your students learning

♥ When you get good feedback from your supervisor

♦ When you inspire others

♣ All the time (whether people agree with you or not!)

♥ Not sure (You are working on it!)

12. When you start a new project, you are likely to:

♥ doubt yourself and feel a bit anxious;

♠ be ambitious and overachieve to impress everyone;

♣ be frustrated to have one more thing on your list;

♦ be excited and ready to start innovating; or

♥ organize yourself to achieve the minimum requirement.

13. In a collaborative project that seems likely to fail, what is your likely attitude?

   ♦ You like challenges, so you will have a dynamic and positive attitude toward this one.
   ♣ You feel like everything is falling apart, so why should you care?
   ♠ You're optimistic, as always! And you'll push everyone to get it done even if the process is ugly and painful.
   ♥ You'll let others take initiative and you'll do your part, but whatever happens happens.
   ♠ You're in charge now! You'll take the lead and get this up and running again.

14. Tomorrow is a professional-development day at your school, so you are:

   ♣ annoyed at another session of wasted time;
   ♠ ready to spend hours researching the topics to be covered, so that you are super ready to participate and show your prior knowledge;
   ♦ looking forward to learning new things and ready to be an active participant;
   ♥ ready to listen and take notes; or
   ♠ overexcited (by the way, you are presenting at multiple sessions!).

15. You have a new boss at your school, and this is your reaction:

   ♦ "I am glad and ready to start collaborating!"
   ♣ "Oh no! A new manager is only going to tell me what to change, and I like the way I'm doing things now."
   ♥ "I will need to find out a little more about this person when she starts…"
   ♠ "I need to google this person immediately, search his/her digital footprint, and then connect with him/her on social media."
   ♣ "Who cares? I'll just mind my own business per usual and hope I won't be bothered."
   ♠ "I think I'll send my new boss an email right away to introduce myself, and I'll include some of my top achievements to impress her."

16. Your colleague is absent and you are covering for him/her. This is how you proceed:

    ◆ You figure out his/her plan and deliver the best possible lesson, as you imagine he/she would have expected.

    ♥ You try to convey the details of the lesson but end up letting students watch a movie.

    ♠ You start with the initial plan but make many decisions as you go to significantly improve it.

    ♣ You just share the scheduled lesson with the students and warn them they better finish the work without speaking and without questions.

17. You see a student who looks depressed. What do you do?

    ♠ You call the counselor right away and email all the teachers with your concerns.

    ♦ You engage with the student gently: "You seem upset. Do you want to talk to me about it?"

    ♣ You ignore the student. (Nowadays, kids just dramatize everything!)

    ◆ You contact this student's best friend, and watch the magic of friendship do its charm.

    ♥ You pass by and continue with your day. The student is not in your class anyway.

18. A colleague comes to you for help with a project. What's your reaction?

    ♥ "I'll just do the work myself. It takes longer to explain what to do than to do it."

    ♣ "I don't have time—sorry!"

    ♦ "Of course! This is a great opportunity to collaborate!"

    ♠ "With some mentoring, I think my experience could really benefit you. Let's schedule several sessions to achieve the best possible outcome."

19. What is your opinion about social media for professional use?

    ♦ It's an outstanding opportunity to learn and grow as a global educator.

- ♠ It's a great tool for marketing oneself and getting a super-duper online reputation!
- ♥ You never remember your password, so you'll probably just join again later, when it's more convenient.
- ♣ It's all about showing off, which is lame and arrogant. You don't get it.
- ♠ You keep tweeting all day long! You are addicted to sharing and viewing!

20. There is a new platform at school, and this is your first impression:

- ♣ You are so angry to have to start over again!
- ♦ You are excited to embrace this change.
- ♥ You are a bit frustrated because it will force you to learn something new, but you will probably get on board eventually.
- ♠ You are already thinking of suggesting additional tools that integrate well with this platform.

Now, go to appendix A to calculate your score and find your profile.

## *Meditation Prompt*

### Reflecting on Your Flexibility as an Educator

This is your first meditation prompt. Take a moment to pause, breathe deeply and slowly, and be present to yourself. This journaling exercise is for you to connect with yourself and reflect on your current context.

After examining your inclination for flexibility through calculating your score and reading the profile(s) that best represent you, how do you think it compares to your expectations of yourself?

_____

_____

_____

## *Edtech Props*

### Learning More about Yourself

If you liked our quiz, you might also like these other online personality quizzes:

✦ "How Much GRIT Do You Have?" voluntary research study at the University of Pennsylvania: sasupenn.qualtrics.com/jfe/form/ SV_06f6QSOS2pZW9qR

✦ Personality Test by NERIS Type Explorer (at 16Personalities.com): 16personalities.com/free-personality-test

## *Inspiration*

### Getting Started on Your Journey

As you embark on this new journey, here are some additional resources to further your learning:

✦ *Rethinking Education in the Age of Technology: The Digital Revolution and Schooling in America* by Allan Collins and Richard Halverson (New York: Teachers College Press, 2009): Read this book to learn about the transformations occuring in education due to the technological revolution.

✦ *Drive: The Surprising Truth About What Motivates Us* by Daniel Pink (New York: Riverhead Books, 2010): This book will make you unleash your growth potential by making you understand what motivation truly is!

✦ *Strengthsfinder 2.0: Discover your CliftonStrengths* by Tom Rath (New York: Gallup Press, 2007): Take the Strengthsfinder assessment to learn more about yourself and your strengths, then use the book as a reference to better understand how to best use your strengths.

# Part 1
# Breathe

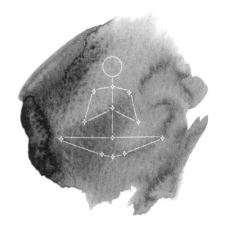

"We are what we repeatedly do. Excellence, then, is not an act but a habit."

—Will Durant, *The Story of Philosophy*

I n yoga, everything is tied to the breath. Each pose is coordinated with the breath. As you move through poses, you breathe in and out, connecting breath and movement. Connecting movement to breath makes the body and mind become one. Breath is the foundation for all other movements. Breath is the force that both revitalizes the body and the mind, allowing yogis to release any tension, and feel calm and relaxed.

In edtech yoga, we also start with the breath. Consider breathing as the vital force that allows you to pause and envision infinite possibilities. The routine of educators often revolves around strict timetables, meetings, noisy environments, and short breaks. In addition, educators are often extremely dedicated human beings who give up their personal time to planning, grading, reflecting, and supporting students or colleagues outside of their regular schedule, taking care of themselves last. Indeed, many will relate to this observation: teachers spend many of their holidays sick at home! Teachers just hold the pressure until the students are off, and when they suddenly release the tension, the body cries for rest! But balance and self-care are absolutely non-negotiable. We need to breathe and make breathing a habit. As you consciously and intentionally breathe, you will feel better and establish clearer vision as a growing educator.

Before you begin your stretching journey, let's take a moment to pause and invest some time in being mindful and present with ourselves. Simply focus on your breathing until you feel calm and connected. Once you feel centered, think about yourself and your goals: What are your strengths and areas of improvement? What goals do you have for technology integration? When you envision the perfect edtech classroom, what does it look like compared to your current classroom? How does your vision impact you, your students, and perhaps your school community or broader professional learning networks?

For your stretching journey, we want you to use this calm and connected space to envision your potential and then put it into action. In chapter one, you will envision the kind of educator you want to become, identify what inspires you, and explore your purpose. In chapter two, you will start to connect your edtech vision to your pedagogy and attitude about edtech as you begin to think about how you might put your vision into action. And in chapter three, you will expand the boundaries of your vision by exploring how you connect with others. (Remember that we will be along for the ride, providing specific strategies and action steps to assist you on your journey.)

# ISTE Standards for Educators that Connect to Part 1

## 1. LEARNER

**Educators continually improve their practice by learning from and with others and exploring proven and promising practices that leverage technology to improve student learning. Educators:**

**1a**

Set professional learning goals to explore and apply pedagogical approaches made possible by technology and reflect on their effectiveness.

**1b**

Pursue professional interests by creating and actively participating in local and global learning networks.

**1c**

Stay current with research that supports improved student learning outcomes, including findings from the learning sciences.

## 2. LEADER

Educators seek out opportunities for leadership to support student empowerment and success and to improve teaching and learning. Educators:

| 2a | 2b | 2c |
|---|---|---|
| Shape, advance, and accelerate a shared vision for empowered learning with technology by engaging with education stakeholders. | Advocate for equitable access to educational technology, digital content, and learning opportunities to meet the diverse needs of all students. | Model for colleagues the identification, exploration, evaluation, curation, and adoption of new digital resources and tools for learning. |

# Envision What Might Be

"You are stronger than you believe. You have greater powers than you know."

—Antiope, character in *Wonder Woman*

In a postindustrial society, it is imperative that students learn the skills necessary to succeed and contribute positively as global citizens in the digital age. As Collins and Halverson (2010) note, technology can and should transform teaching and learning. A more recent indication of the critical need for effective and meaningful technology integration in schools is evident in the 2016 National Education Technology Plan, which states that technology integration is critical to teaching, learning, leadership, assessment, and infrastructure.

Chapter one begins with the demystification of technology integration so that you have the freedom to think about best practices for edtech. Then we establish a postconstructivist approach as our philosophy toward learning. (With this philosophy in hand, our hope is that you'll remember you are not alone in this exploration of designing your emerging "you.") Next, we share specific strategies for doing this, including walking through a visible thinking routine, finding your "om," becoming a "glocal" educator, engaging in self-analysis, and examining the value of developing a network. Finally, we show you how to meet your emerging self so that you can start your journey toward action and growth.

You picked up this book to become a better educator. You may be looking for ways to be innovative, for encouragement to re-energize yourself and your classroom, or for new ideas for integrating technology into your classroom in ways that make sense. But it all comes down to change and a willingness to pursue and embrace it.

## Understanding and Designing Your Emerging "You"

Let's pause and breathe together. It's time to take a step back, gain some distance from the present, and think about what we might be able to create. Often, we set goals that follow a linear approach. Instead of creating linear and conclusive goals, what about casting aside a prescribed template and approaching personalized learning in a more organic way? George Couros (2015) says that innovation is "creating something new and better" (p. 19). *Better* is the important piece of Couros's statement. Think about person- alized learning as a way to become a better educator. What if we became aware of our unknown self and of all the possibilities that lie in this inner zone? What could happen then? In this chapter, let's acknowledge the people and ideas that inspire us; but instead of trying to mold ourselves to what we think is expected to "look" innovative, we will explore what matters most to us and discover our voice and our better selves. As Simon Sinek (2011) says, "If you don't know WHY, you can't know HOW" (p. 70). Your WHY is your purpose, which determines your authenticity and uniqueness.

We hope that as you read this book, you feel a sense of starting fresh. This fresh start might be a way to reconsider your insight and your teaching practices. It might even change the way you see yourself as an educator.

To help you discover the best version of your educator self, we created the following mindfulness meditation. To perform this exercise, you will need to have your eyes closed; so you can either ask someone to read the text to you, or you can go to the the video (noborderslearning.com/stretch-yourself) and listen to the instructions there. During this experience, be gentle with your- self. Let go of the things you are not satisfied with, and welcome the positive thoughts that emerge. Suspend any negative thoughts and concentrate on what is in front of you: your dream and vision of the perfect classroom. No matter your current environment, this meditation will bring you closer to your best version as an educator.

# Stretching Exercise

### Discovering Your Best Version as an Educator: A Mindfulness Meditation

Find a quiet space where you can sit or lie down (on your back) comfortably. If you're sitting, place your hands on your thighs; if you're lying down, place your arms away from your body. Close your eyes and let your body rest. Concentrate on your breathing: inhale and exhale slowly; breathe in and breathe out. Become aware of the feelings in your body as you continue to inhale and exhale at your own pace. Feel your breathing beginning to calm you down—slowly, gently. Bring your awareness to the movements of your abdomen rising up and down. Release all tension from your body and feel your muscles relax. Feel the contact points of your body with the surface you are sitting or lying on. Bring your attention to your shoulders, slowly letting go of any remaining tension.

Now that you are relaxed, let's take a learning journey together.

Imagine that you are on a magic carpet, gently floating in the air. You feel calm, and there is a light breeze carrying you toward the perfect classroom.

Enter the classroom door and begin to soak in the space. Pay attention to the light coming through the windows. This first impression makes you feel welcome, safe, and content. Take in the positive vibrations of the room. There is soothing music in the air—it's not too dim, nor is it too loud.

Look at the key elements of the classroom. The walls are a light color; student work is displayed with clarity and intention. You see the importance of student voices and choices and how the showcase is about sharing the learning process.

There are diverse seating arrangements, with seats of different sizes and shapes that allow flexibility and are integrated in harmony with the space, providing choices and mobility for various activities.

All the colors in the classroom work together to create the right stimulation for learning.

As you continue to observe the space, you invite students to appear in it. When they enter the classroom, they bring in their positive energy. You can feel their excitement and readiness to learn.

The students interact with one another collaboratively. They build a sense of togetherness, cooperation, and interdependence through nonverbal communication and appropriation of space. Because they decide on their learning paths deliberately, they model responsibility. While they dare to innovate by taking risks, with caution, you feel delighted to see them test solutions and persevere. You see them being present to their iterations, self-evaluating and self-correcting.

As they engage in their learning experiences, you see them create with technology. They demonstrate their learning in different ways, choosing the tools that best support their purpose. As they engage in solving challenges with peers, they prepare to share ideas with the entire class. In doing so, they inspire one another.

Take a moment to look at the students from a distance, visiting different learning groups around the room. As you zoom in and out by moving on your magic carpet, look at the students from different perspectives.... How are the students engaged in their learning? What is the balance of students' independence and interdependence? How are students sharing their learning? You feel happy and satisfied observing learning in action.

Now, imagine that this effervescent classroom is yours. You are the teacher, leading and co-learning.

Gently lower your carpet to the floor like a leaf floating down to a bed of grass. As you reach the floor, feel your feet touch the ground, and take your place in this scene.

Your students notice your presence and greet you. You serenely return their greeting and move around the classroom to interact with different groups. You are intentional in the way you prioritize. You see which groups are working independently and which ones need your feedback. You are aware that certain students respond more effectively than others to your feedback, and you adjust your words and nonverbal language to best support their growth. You stop and actively listen to some of the students as they work, and you feel a deep sense of fulfilment as you witness the learning taking shape as desired.

We are now completing our journey in this mediation. It's time to distance yourself from the details.

Return to your carpet and take a relaxed pose on it. Slowly bring your attention back to your body and to your breathing. Breathe in and out slowly. Feel the peaceful presence that remains from your meditative practice; and when you are ready, open your eyes and come back to your physical surroundings and this book.

## *Meditation Prompt*

### Your Educational Beliefs

You just explored your vision of the dream classroom and imagined your best version as an educator. Take a moment to reflect on this experience. What are some of the values that emerged from your exploration? What are the most important beliefs you hold as a teacher? Write down your thoughts about what drives you to be an educator, keeping the big picture in mind.

_____

_____

_____

_____

_____

_____

_____

_____

_____

_____

_____

_____

## Being Present Is Crucial

Through both of the meditation exercises you just performed, you might have realized that being present with the students and with yourself is crucial. We need to be conscious of what is happening around us and within us. If we consciously attend to ourselves and others, we can make better decisions and mold ourselves to fit the ideal image we have of ourselves—one sculpted by best practices. The key is to allow ourselves to genuinely and consciously take the time to pause and observe instead of rushing to act, and then worrying after the fact about what could have been done better.

It's not helpful to focus on the past, which will always have bits of dissatisfaction that cannot be changed. However, we *do* have the power to monitor and change ourselves to be who we want to be in *the here and now.* We can create our future as forward thinkers starting this very moment. Of course, there is a level of vulnerability in being attuned to the present; while we might have a goal in mind for a particular lesson, that goal might change. We may not be able to rely on the reassurance and confidence of a well-crafted lesson plan. Fortunately, being reflective educators will help us to trigger learning and aha moments for our students. By being flexible, we can grasp opportunities that we did not foresee.

## Finding Your Edtech "Om"

"Om" is a common mantra in yoga that signifies ultimate consciousness or reality. The purpose of om or any mantra is to help center your actions, thoughts, and emotions. It's a sound that you utter and creates a vibration inside you. Some yogis find it daunting to let out their om because it can seem odd in the beginning; however, when we let ourselves be open-minded, we realize that suspending our judgments and ignoring the "noises" inside our head allows us to embrace a new way of being. In edtech yoga, what is your centering mantra? What vision(s) make you feel calm, hopeful, or peaceful? What might be the phrase that resonates in you? As you develop your own vision and become increasingly aware of your beliefs and values as an educator, you'll witness and appreciate the clarity it brings. Having a clear vision helps you set goals and create a path for yourself.

As you think about your vision of edtech, think about what inspires you. What could be an ideal image, inspiring quote, or driving motto for you? You'll use this as your om—your reminder of what is important to you. You'll use it to support you in difficult times, a reminder to step back and take a deep breath. This practice will allow you to see the big picture before you investigate specific discomforts up close.

To discover what inspires you, work through the following stretching exercise. As a result of the process, you'll create a collage that's a visual reminder of your inspirations.

# Stretching Exercise

## Creating an Inspirational Collage

This exercise will help you reflect on what is important to you, what requires attention to improve your practice, what to strive for, and how to regain motivation when you are down by making your thinking visible. It is a useful activity that both adults and children can enjoy and benefit from. It is also a nice warm-up learning experience in a meeting or professional-development session.

As demonstrated in the following diagram, you have six elements to fill in with visuals and/or words. These visuals can be pasted or written on this very page, or ideally, you can make yourself a larger version to keep in your classroom or office—somewhere you can see it every day to keep up your spirits and to emphasize what matters to you. And you might decide to change the content of the collage as time goes on, if your priorities change.

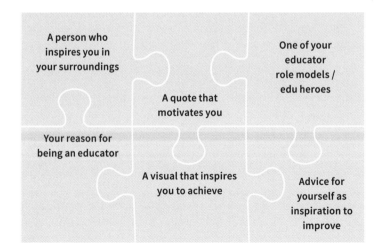

# Rethinking the "Tech" in Edtech

When you think of edtech, your first thought might be edtech tools, such as apps and websites, or other gadgets and materials we use in makerspaces. However, we are moving toward technology as a way to learn, create, and share ideas. It's time to see technology as a means to innovate.

Before the 20th century, classroom instructional materials mostly consisted of the blackboard, the teacher, and textbooks. Then, the 20th century brought new technologies, like projectors, radio, television, and finally, the computer, in the 1980s. The computer had the potential to revolutionize the classroom because it offered innovative features; with this new device, students and teachers could interact, collaborate, create, and learn. Now, with the advent of the internet, students and teachers can interact within a global learning environment that supports connected global citizens. The internet has opened up a new world because what it offers isn't something that can be quantified or touched; it allows its users to access an immense array of information within a few clicks—an infinite sense of freedom and possibilities. The internet is not a thing; it's a concept—abstract yet real! Moving from a device-oriented reality to an intangible realm, technology has become ubiquitous and versatile.

Let's think about technology skill levels for a minute. You might picture all students as being tech savvy (though that's not always the case, because it depends on their exposure), and you might compare tech-savvy teachers to the traditional teachers within your community. But educator Tonia A. Dousay (assistant professor of learning sciences and researcher at the Doceo Center for Innovation + Learning, University of Idaho) shares this realization with us: "You're as savvy as you need to be. You know what you need to know, when you need it, and how you need it. When you need to learn something new, you find the resources to fill the gap."

Some educators might hold the idea that technology is forced on us because we live in the digital age, but it's our choice to make technology relevant to us. We need to be able to recognize when we need to direct and teach ourselves a new tech skill. We encourage you to think of technology as an opportunity, with infinite possibilities for learning.

# Embracing Edtech Stewardship

We often hear assertive statements in education, and sometimes, they sound black or white. Stances come at full force and don't allow much space for understanding or perspectives. While divergent thinking and conflicts of ideas are always welcome for educators to keep their fire, their purpose is not to disrupt for the sake of it, or to give a platform for complaint, victimization, and sulking. Battles do not really help anyone move forward. Instead of always seeing educational issues as a competition, how could we use them as a learning model for our students?

The mission of the International Society for Technology in Education (ISTE) is as follows:

> ISTE inspires educators worldwide to use technology to innovate teaching and learning, accelerate good practice and solve tough problems in education by providing community, knowledge and the ISTE Standards, a framework for rethinking education and empowering learners.

Sometimes, as educators, we consider ourselves disruptors. The problem is that the disruptor comes with a know-it-all reputation, and that's not what we want. What we really want is to take fellow educators and students with us on a learning quest, but we want to avoid doing this forcefully. Michelle Cordy, a teacher at Thames Valley District School Board in London, Ontario, gave a keynote at ISTE 2016, in which she told us, "Because schools aren't broken, and we are not here to fix them, I don't think we need to break them down and rebuild them." She continued by stating that "schools and districts are ecosystems, and ecosystems don't break. But we do need to take care of them."

So how might we embrace the stewardship of best practices for edtech integration in the classroom? Stewardship is not about leading change and building changemakers; it's about celebrating learning. Innovation is likely to occur in pockets and not across an entire school all at once, for instance, but however it occurs, time, perseverance, and effort are needed for transformation. One person alone cannot control the pace of change. Empowerment is never something that you can teach people; it is something that every individual needs to build for themselves. Even so, an empowered person can offer a great deal of inspiration to others around her or him.

In order to usher other educators or our learners toward empowerment, we need to start with an awareness of new learning opportunities. Do people know there is something new to learn? Sometimes we assume that people have gone through this first step, but that might not be the case. As educator-leaders, we need to facilitate this awareness that there is something new to learn. Once people are aware and committed to the journey, we can begin to think about next steps in learning.

Included in the mission of ISTE are the essential conditions for edtech implementation. It's about the transformation of mindset through actions. We must ensure that we are going to take a holistic view of edtech that includes not just training and coaching but policy making, planning, reflecting, and the constant need for improvement. The ISTE mission also embraces lifelong learning that brings people together. The mission prioritizes building interconnected networks of personal learning.

## Challenges for Learning

What challenges do you face?

In our profession, we face many challenges, both in the classroom and in the larger educational environment. There are so many external factors (e.g., curriculum, policies, rules, standardized testing, lack of funding) that can make us feel trapped and powerless. When these circumstances directly impact your job or your classroom, it is truly a challenge. For example, we know that data collection can provide us with a wealth of information about how students learn best. As with any educational trend, however, it can be taken too far. Documenting every little thing can be cumbersome, and to what end? Is it truly informing our teaching and learning to create best practices, or are we documenting simply to follow the latest trends?

All of these external constraints may seem daunting, or even overwhelming, but there is a way out: we can focus on the factors that we can control and also how we respond to challenging situations.

Teaching can be a strenuous profession, particularly when you are new to the field or when you are trying to stretch yourself and your students. Change is hard, and you will undoubtedly face the challenges of change as an educator. But don't despair! You can and will overcome these challenges. Knowing what is coming and what you are already facing makes it easier to develop strategies to overcome these difficult situations—an important step in this journey. What are some of the ways you could assess challenges? How could you learn to recognize the difference between internal and external challenges?

One of the ways to assess challenges might be to let them out or expose them by simply listing their negative aspects. Or you might prefer to talk through them or share them with a friend to receive support. Whatever way you choose to let them out will probably help a great deal toward making you feel lighter, as acknowledging the existence of these challenges makes them less scary and opens the door to finding solutions.

Self-reflection might also be a worthy component of assessing challenges, as you know yourself the best. Allow yourself to be open to feedback from others, whether it is from your students, your colleagues, or your broader professional learning community. As mentioned earlier, the first step of learning is the very awareness that there is something new to be learned. It can be difficult to do but worth it, because feedback from others can better define what challenges you might face. However well you know yourself and your situation, feedback from others provides diverse perspectives that can lead to better solutions.

For another way to look at challenges, work through the following "Turning It Upside Down!" stretching exercise.

# Stretching Exercise

## Turning It Upside Down!

Sometimes challenges feel insurmountable. When you are running out of solutions and feel stuck, one way to unlock the problem might be to look at it from another perspective. This approach is inspired by the game Reverse It from Donna Spencer (UX Mastery, n.d.).

The strategy is simple: disrupt your thinking. To get unstuck, think about the opposite of your problem—turn it upside down. For example, if your problem is a lack of resources, think about the problem of having access to too many resources! You might feel overwhelmed by the choices and, as such, never feel content with what you choose. You might not develop the same skills with students, as having access to everything might breed a lack of perseverance that causes students to go for the solution that looks easy but doesn't solve the problem.

As you then try to brainstorm ideas to solve the reverse problem, you might list things such as *declutter, give away stuff, keep only what is important.*

In the process of generating these ideas, you will slowly come to realize that the problem likely lies somewhere else, revealing the true learning value as well as your true intentions. In the case of limited resources, you might become aware of the importance of focusing on the concept to teach rather than on the gadget to buy. Thanks to the internet, you can find a lot of alternatives to address limited access to resources; you might find a website that helps you simulate a robotics scenario instead of having to buy a robot, or you could watch a DIY tutorial to create a cardboard model of a robotics system that's equally helpful toward meeting your teaching goal.

Now, it's your turn!

1. Identify the problem:

_____

_____

_____

_____

_____

2. Reverse it:

_____

_____

_____

_____

3. What solutions could solve your reverse problem?

_____

_____

_____

4. What did you become aware of about your initial problem after you brain-stormed ideas for solving the reverse problem?

## Visible Thinking: A Routine

Visible thinking routines are excellent step-by-step processes that support us in clarifying and deepening our thinking about our content as well as our own thinking skills. For example, a routine could identify what we already know about a topic while revealing what we want to know next.

The next stretching exercise takes you through a helpful visible thinking routine. You might also want to browse through the different visible thinking routines and other teaching and learning resources available from Harvard's Project Zero (goo .gl/q92K3e), or you can scan the QR code to the right:

Project Zero is all about understanding learning through various means (by integrating various intellectual aspects such as creativity, thinking, understanding, and ethics) through the arts. The project continues to grow and connects more elements that inspire an inter- and trans-disciplinary approach.

# Stretching Exercise

## Walking Through a Visible Thinking Routine

Let's try the popular visible thinking routine "See, Think, Wonder" (Ritchhart, Church, & Morrison, 2011) using "The Iceberg Illusion" illustration, which encapsulates the concept of success. The purpose of this routine is to make mindful observations that stimulate inquiry and curiosity.

Look at the picture and write your notes under "I see…" by focusing on what you observe about the image. It's important to do this first before completing the other boxes so you really look closely at the details of the image. One tip might be to imagine that you are describing this image to a person who cannot see it. Take your time to look closely. Then proceed to the next phase, "I think…" where you might make connections to certain concepts and take the essence of the image into a broadened context or your own context. Finally, fill

Reproduced with the permission of Sylvia Duckworth (2016, p. 49).

in the "I wonder…" box by letting yourself ask questions, make inferences, and connect to your context, allowing you to investigate your own ideas further.

And remember, there are no wrong answers, so just go for it!

| I see… | I think… | I wonder… |
| --- | --- | --- |
| | | |

How does the "See, Think, Wonder" visual thinking routine help us stretch ourselves? When you are able to see, think, and wonder, you better understand where you are coming from and what it is that you actually want to achieve. According to Sinek (2011), "Achievement happens when we pursue and attain WHAT we want. Success comes when we are in clear pursuit of WHY we want it." (p. 181) He also explains the difference between achievement and success: while achievement is something you attain (like a goal), success is a feeling or a state of being. We want you to feel successful and own it!

## *Take a Breath*

### Celebrate Every Success!

If you are a big fan of using Post-it Notes to write yourself reminders or to-do lists, consider storing your completed Post-it Notes in a box. At the end of the week, month, term, and academic year, open the box. Congratulate yourself on all that you have accomplished in that time!

Consider doing this with your students as well. Have students write down their accomplishments on Post-it Notes and provide a bulletin board in your classroom where students can share them with their classmates. By the end of the year, the wall will be full of inspiration and things to celebrate!

## Finding Your Big WHY and Setting Up Your Goals

We often focus on giving information, but what if we focused on questions for ourselves instead? Questions stretch us by inviting us to inquire (Wood Brooks & John, 2018), a means through which we can explore the big picture or zoom in to see the details. Looking at our questions from multiple angles and perspectives allows us to grow.

One way to use this questioning process is in finding your purpose—your big WHY. For that, let's get some inspiration from the Japanese concept of *ikigai*, translated as "the happiness of always being busy" (Garcia & Miralles, 2016) and also described by many as "the reason we get up in the morning."

*Ikigai* encompasses the idea that our purpose is determined by the intersection of our passion, mission, vocation, and profession. Therefore, to live and breathe our *ikigai*, we need to answer four questions:

✦ When I combine my passion and my mission, what do I love doing?

✦ When I combine my mission and my vocation, what does the world need that I can offer?
✦ When I combine my vocation and my profession, what can I be paid to do?
✦ When I combine my profession and my passion, what am I good at?

(Winn, 2014)

Now, it's your turn to explore your *ikigai* in the following stretching exercise.

# Stretching Exercise

## Identifying Your *Ikigai*

Reveal your own *ikigai* by answering the four questions about your passion, your mission, your vocation, and your profession and then placing your keywords in each of the corresponding parts of the following chart.

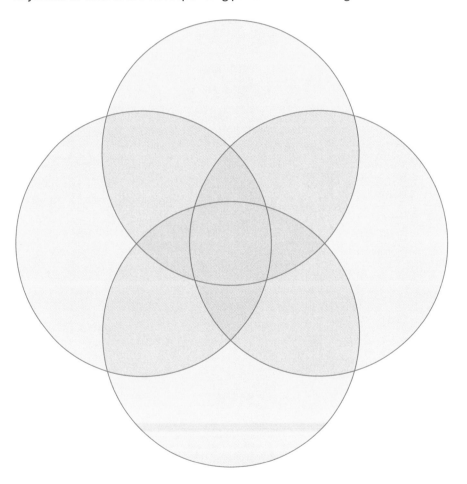

Now that you've found your WHY, think further about your vision by completing one or both of the activities in the following stretching exercise. Your choice!

# *Stretching Exercise*

## Embodying Your Vision

### Choice 1—The Power of Authority

When you introduce yourself, you might want to skip the usual "I am a teacher," and instead, find a creative, powerful, and assertive tagline that best encapsulates your purpose, passion, and drive. Try to incorporate your WHY (belief, values, identity, cause, or reason).

Here are a few examples of taglines:

✦ I am a people empowerer
✦ I am an avid inquirer
✦ I am a serial-mistake maker and iterator!

There is something powerful and transformative about writing down these things about ourselves—when you write it, you become it! And this tagline can become a tagline for your professional social media as well. Use the lines below to start brainstorming!

_____

_____

_____

_____

_____

*(continued on next page)*

### Choice 2—Elevator Pitch

Create an elevator pitch to put your big WHY into writing. Fill in the template below with your own words. Feel free to change the template or create your pitch from scratch. (A few examples have been provided to model this exercise.)

**As a/an** _____**, my aim is to**

_____ **so that learners can have/feel/be**

_____ **and** _____ .

Examples:

✦ As a **committed educator**, my aim is to **facilitate learning** so that learners can **shine** and **achieve**.

✦ As an **empowered learner and leader**, my aim is to **challenge myself** so that learners can **have a role model to look up to** and **be determined and persistent in learning**.

✦ As a **changemaker**, my aim is to **keep trying new things** so that learners **can feel safe to make mistakes**, **can iterate and develop persistence**, and **can keep improving**.

## Meeting Your Emerging Self

Before you continue on to chapter two, where you'll put your vision into action, we have one more stretching exercise to help you jump-start your change process.

# Stretching Exercise

## Exploring Your Vision by Recording a Video of Yourself

Go back to basics by making a video of your current teaching practice—a straightforward collection of data—and examine the results. This is all you need to do:

1. Videotape your next lesson. Don't plan a fancy lesson; just videotape your usual lesson.

2. Once you have your recording, follow these steps:

   A. Immediately following the lesson, answer this question: How did it go?

   B. Now watch the video of yourself and answer the question again, based on the evidence and data in front of you.

3. Based on your response to the video, please do one of the following:

   A. If your answer was roughly positive, great! It's always a good feeling to have a lesson that went well. However, since this book is about stretching your practice, can you think of any ways that you might expand on your lesson or extend student learning even further? Brainstorm a list of ideas for taking your great lesson to the next level, making it even greater!

   B. If your answer was roughly negative, that's okay—nobody is perfect. What specifically went wrong? Brainstorm a list of specific strategies that you could use to improve the lesson the next time around.

4. Finally, reflect on the following questions:

   A. What did you learn about yourself during this exercise?

   B. What commitments might you make to modify your practice the next time you encounter a similar pattern?

*Inspiration*

## Focusing on Your Purpose

Here are some additional resources to further your learning of this new way of thinking and being:

✦ *Good to Great: Why Some Companies Make the Leap…and Others Don't* by Jim Collins (New York: HarperCollins, 2001): Collins uses years of research studying successful businesses to discover the keys to success, including strategies for addressing leadership, management, competence, culture, and radical change.

✦ *Start with Why: How Great Leaders Inspire Everyone to Take Action* by Simon Sinek (New York: The Penguin Group, 2011): This is a popular book that keeps reminding us to always start with the WHY (our reasons, our purpose), as knowing this helps us to achieve and inspire.

## Put Your Vision into Action

"I learned this, at least, by my experiment: that if one advances confidently in the direction of his dreams, and endeavors to live the life which he has imagined, he will meet with a success unexpected in common hours."

—Henry David Thoreau, *Walden; Or, Life in the Woods*

You envisioned what could be in chapter one, hopefully with a feeling of "can" rather than "can't." In this chapter, you will learn how to implement your vision and make it actionable; or, in yoga terms, connect your mind (vision) to your body (action).

We'll start by establishing a postconstructivist approach as our philosophy toward learning. Then we'll present two approaches to help you find the courage to be your emerging "you." Each of these approaches will show you how to stay calm, be aware, and be inclusive. Finally, we discuss the value of doing more with less and the importance of confidence, particularly when you are stretching and putting yourself out there. As you develop your craft to make your vision possible and real, you will need agility and resources (including human resources).

## A Postconstructivist Approach

It's important to understand how students learn in order to better develop your approach to teaching. The constructivist perspective has its foundations in the philosophical and psychological theories developed by educational theorists like Jean Piaget in the early 20th century (Ertmer & Newby, 1993). The main tenet of constructivism is that knowledge and learning are constructed through the process of "meaning making": based on context, prior knowledge, and active learning. In constructivism, learning is personal—it is dependent on the learner, the learner's experiences, and the learner's construction of new knowledge.

Through his phenomenological perspective, Wolff-Michael Roth (2015) proposes the postconstructivist theory that learning might not be constructed but rather the result of *becoming aware*. When we think about the learning process, do we conceptualize the act of learning as a step-by-step construction or more as an epiphany? Roth believes that this moment of awareness is not constructed but organic and spontaneous. When students follow instructions and complete them successfully, we could argue that they are not actually learning anything new; but don't we feel ourselves learning when we have an aha moment, even if the conditions for that aha moment are manufactured? While the constructivist theory of Piaget implies that one knows where one is heading, Roth proposes the idea that one may not know what the result might be. We believe that both constructivism and postconstructivism are approaches to learning that have value, as they make us constantly examine how our students learn.

So, while we try to trigger learning by creating conditions that *might* provoke awarenesses, it is better to develop our presence in the classroom— to observe and provide feedback in the moment to facilitate those aha moments. For example, you could provide a task that students are *almost* able to do; watch them troubleshoot a solution; and provide feedback in the form of questions, comments, or nonverbal cues.

We also need to realize that too much "teacher talk" can prevent students from learning. When teachers spend most of their time talking, students literally do not have a voice! As educators, it is a good idea to observe ourselves in the classroom and reflect on our "talk quota." If we really want to create an atmosphere where students have the opportunity to construct their own meaningful learning, we need to regulate ourselves by teaching less to "let learn" more. Students who only receive information from the teacher become passive members of the classroom rather than active participants. Teacher talk puts the teacher, not the students, in control of the learning.

Caleb Gattegno says that "communication is almost a miracle" (1976/2010, 60–61), and indeed, we don't always understand one another when we express ourselves. Educator Rushton Hurley (from NextVista.org, author of *Making Your Teaching Something Special*) shared his insights with us: "It's not about what you say; it's about what they hear." He sums up the idea that communication happens for a purpose, but that purpose might not always be heard by the receiver of the message. The point to remember here: apply agility when communicating by using modalities other than communication.

In the 1950s, Gattegno formalized various teaching practices into a coherent whole that he called "the subordination of teaching to learning" (Gattegno, 1987a and 1987b). This principle revolves around the idea that teachers need to have a clear understanding of how learning occurs. The role of the teacher is not to explain or to provide a model to memorize and repeat but to create visible and tangible situations in which *awarenesses* can be triggered.

Gattegno (1977) often talked about awareness in its plural form, particularly within learning. First, one must become aware of opportunities for learning new things; and then, one must be present within the learning experience to experiment and explore. Only through interacting with content, making mistakes, and trying new things can we truly become aware of what there is to learn; experience is what makes learning a more automatic process—one that requires less attention to activate new knowledge. The final level of awareness in learning is being able to transfer learned knowledge to new situations. Once we are aware of how to transfer knowledge, we can activate it for the rest of our lives.

Some of the specifics of this approach were later described and expanded upon by Roslyn Young and Piers Ruston Messum (2011); and in the following four sections, we have adopted and adapted their four learning phases to focus on personalized learning for educators.

✦ Phase 1: Be aware that there is something new to be learned.

This phase is simple but not simplistic. Have you noticed that we don't know what we don't know? That means we aren't aware yet of the awarenesses that await us! This phase really means that the first step to learning is to become aware that there is indeed something new to learn. Occasionally, the new learning happens in a place of discomfort, particularly when we have to unlearn! We must bring our presence to the unknown and realize that there is something new to be learned.

✦ Phase 2: Explore through trial and error.

We hear it all over the edtech sphere: we need to let ourselves and our students fail, yet let's insist that the outcome is *not* to fail! The outcome is *learning*, but we invite errors to the table. Making errors and taking risks teach us resilience and persistence, and they spark curiosity. But it's not the risks and the errors that we need to focus on; the most important part is the feedback we receive from the environment in which we are exploring new situations or from our peers. When we are present with this feedback, we find our next steps, we iterate, and we realize what to adjust in order to improve. It's always scary to ride a bicycle the first time, but do you remember the feeling when you got back on the bike after a few falls and you finally felt that you were balanced and in control? The feeling of achievement was real and yours alone.

✦ Phase 3: Practice until it's automatized.

We realize that by mastering the art of being fully present with the latest piece of the learning puzzle, we appropriate our new learning completely. As we practice this new thing we've learned, however, we eventually eliminate the need to bring our awareness, because we have learned and automatized this new skill or information. Just like we don't need to think about how to balance on our bicycle once we've learned how to ride it, we will be able to take our presence to new learning situations once other newly learned skills have become second nature.

✦ Phase 4: Transfer to another learning situation.

The more we learn, the more we are able to learn! Let's think about it: the different skills we build throughout our experiences support our next learning experiences. For instance, if we speak several languages, it becomes easier for us to speak one more. This is because we can compare and contrast our past learning experiences to make connections and be more flexible—and receptive—in our ongoing approach to learning. Also, we know that learning a language worked in the past, so why not now? Transference in learning is the ability to easily move from one learning scenario to the next and connect the dots faster. Some people think certain individuals are naturally talented because they learn anything new very quickly, but we believe that this has more to do with all the things that might not be visible to others, like previous learning experiences, perseverance, and a tinkering mindset.

## Embracing the Digital Age

Trying to keep up with technology is like drinking from a firehose: it's impossible to keep up with it all! But keeping up is not the goal. Instead, it's about focusing on what you want students to learn and what you want the classroom learning experience to be like. Think about how technology can help you achieve your teaching and learning goals. There will be tools that you won't use in your classroom, and there might even be times that you don't use technology at all. Rather than focusing on the "shiny," let's focus on the learning.

The idea of digital-age learning is that we need to be present in the here and now, and we have the responsibility (and the right!) to welcome and embrace the new. Like educator John Gary Garcia (teacher at Saint Pedro Poveda College in the National Capital Region, Philippines) says, "We cannot teach the way we were taught." Let's be aware of our possible bias due to our past experiences as learners, and let's be present with what is best for our learners and ourselves as innovators *today*.

## Finding the Courage to Be Your Emerging "You"

Now that you have envisioned *what might be*, let's move forward. You might be a bit nervous or scared about your next steps or about how you might achieve your goals, but don't fret! This chapter will help you find the courage to be your emerging "you." Additionally, you will think about ways that you can make deliberate plans and utilize certain strategies to help you find your "can-do power."

So, what exactly is your can-do power? If you feel comfortable within, then you will feel more confident in your abilities to stretch and go beyond your current state. When you have peace, you have power; therefore, inner peace is your can-do power.

Now, you are probably thinking, "Okay, that sounds great, but how do I develop inner peace?" We'll start with the following three approaches, which will give you a healthy boost along your path to power.

### Approach 1: Don't panic!

We thought about writing "Don't panic!" on the cover of this book, but that gimmick was already taken. Instead, we included it as an approach to finding peace.

We know you are a motivated educator and you want to do well, so any complications or failures are likely to seem out of hand, ramping up anxiety levels. But when challenges inevitably arise, here's the first thing you need to remember: *Don't panic!* Remain calm, take a deep breath, and know that this, too, shall pass. When you stay calm, you have power. You may not be able to change the current situation in your classroom, your school, or your district, but you do have the power to change your attitude, your mindset, and your reaction to the situation. Focus your energy on building up the courage to continue forward in the face of difficulties.

Mantras can also keep you calm. Use the following meditation prompt to develop your own personal serenity mantra. (For inspiration, think of phrases like, "I am a confident, strong individual," "This too shall pass," "I can get through this," or simply, "Don't panic!")

## Meditation Prompt

### Personal Mantras

When it comes to keeping calm, what might be some of your personal mantras?

_____

_____

_____

_____

_____

_____

_____

_____

_____

_____

_____

You can also ask yourself self-reflective questions, such as, "Will this matter in an hour? A week? A year?" and "Will I remember this incident or situation when I am retired and looking back on my career?" Often, asking these types of questions will help you realize that a situation is not as dire or as traumatic as it may seem in the moment.

## Approach 2: Be aware of and respond to your surroundings with compassion.

When we talk about _empathy_, we are talking about a human emotion. Having empathy means that we can relate to other humans. When we talk about _compassion_, we are talking about turning empathy into action. The main difference is that empathy is passive while compassion requires action. Beyond being just aware of the emotions and experiences of others, you are proactive, responding in a positive way to make a difference in their lives.

In his TEDx Talk, Nipun Mehta (2012) talks about _giftivism_, which is "the practice of radically generous acts that change the world." He also develops the concept of unleashing our "generosity capital," guiding us through four shifts that need to occur within ourselves in order to impact the world positively through practicing generosity:

1.  A shift from consumption to contribution, in which we appreciate what we received, and with this awareness, feel grateful and help forward.

2. A shift from transaction to trust, in which we stop focusing on what we alone can get and start relying on the power of interconnectedness.

3. A shift from isolation to community, in which we understand that the way we connect with others changes the manifestation of the end product and, therefore, starts cultivating deeper ties.

4. A shift from scarcity to abundance, in which we understand that we actually have enough to meet our needs and discover we can decrease our consumption and increase our contribution to truly experience gratitude.

In other words, being a *giftivist* is driven by our inner desire to behave selflessly, fostering the understanding that there is more to value than money or external recognition, and that creating synergy and bonds with other humans is priceless, encouraging the desire to give rather than to receive. Mehta also mentions that through this attitude, we realize that we should not judge others but, rather, tap into their inner transformational powers. If we make that inner change ourselves, we are very likely to impact the outer world positively.

Now that we know the difference between empathy and compassion, and have explored the power of giftivism, how might we put this into practice to make a positive impact around us? Begin with self-compassion, something you can easily explore by keeping a diary or perhaps a gratitude journal. The following stretching exercise is a self-compassion practice inspired by Kristin Neff (2018).

# Stretching Exercise

## Practicing Self-Compassion

Think of a time in your teaching career when you were angry or disappointed with yourself. What were the circumstances that caused you to feel this way? Write down the specific details about how this transpired and how it made you feel.

_____

_____

_____

_____

After reflecting on your negative self-thought, write a paragraph or two expressing compassion or understanding toward yourself. Imagine what a kind and compassionate friend might say to you if you confided in her or him about your experience.

_____

_____

_____

_____

Now write a few sentences or a paragraph about how you might change or improve in the future—how you might learn from this experience. Then commend yourself and your learning curve and let go of your negative thoughts.

_____

_____

_____

_____

When you start making self-compassion a habit, you model an attitude that you would like others to develop for themselves. When working with students, we always aim to develop individuals who take care of themselves, and are confident and healthy. In order to inspire balanced individuals, we have to ensure that we are balanced too. Then we can fully explore how *our* gifts can best contribute to our learners realizing and sharing *their* gifts, creating a cycle of deep connection to those inner transformative powers that can make a real difference.

## Approach 3: Appreciate and address diverse student needs and perspectives.

As educators, we must develop inclusive classrooms that serve *all* students. Our classrooms contain a diverse group of individuals who bring different backgrounds, experiences, socioemotional needs, and perspectives. Just like in a yoga class, the teacher needs to know her/his students (whether they have physical limitations or are particularly agile and require extensions) so the teaching can adapt and everyone can be challenged. This is how personalized learning works; we look for the right challenge for each person. However, even if we want to be inclusive, we may not know or have access to the right tools for creating an inclusive classroom. You might be interested in various aspects of inclusive practices, such as supporting English learners and providing learning support for students with special needs (whether lower abilities or gifted and talented). Cultural diversity is another consideration in our approach to inclusion.

One way to embrace inclusion is to design your classroom environment to promote a socially and emotionally safe space. For example, you can (1) make a calm-down glitter jar or two, promoting breathing exercises with a simple prop that students can swirl around to the rhythm of their inhalations and exhalations; (2) keep headphones and a simple MP3 player of mindfulness meditations or calming music for students to listen to; (3) gather together (and periodically refresh) a small stack of age-appropriate books to allow students to browse or read; or (4) provide some paper, markers, and pencils for tracing, drawing, and writing projects. Most of these ideas are very easy to implement and can be stored in a little corner of the classroom that's dedicated to creating such an atmosphere. Co-designing the learning environment with students is the most powerful way for them to take ownership, build a rapport with them, and be transparent about how we might address needs together. Indeed, the best resource is often our leaners! Beyond these add-ons, the true meaning of inclusive classrooms can be summed up in the implementation of personalized learning through inquiry. Kath Murdoch (kathmurdoch.com.au) provides excellent resources that guide teachers in including everyone and reaching out to each learner, for example, through the intentional use of language to scaffold our questions for each learner.

The following edtech props feature helpful organizations and strategies focused on understanding diverse student needs and creating warm, welcoming spaces for *all* students.

## Edtech Props

### Cultural Diversity in the Classroom

Check out these resources that promote cultural diversity in the classroom:

✦ Edutopia has a great list called "Preparing for Cultural Diversity: Resources for Teachers." See more at: tinyurl.com/ycuhv4oy.

✦ In the United States, the National Association for Multicultural Education (NAME) has a conference research journal, and resources related to social justice and equity in education. See more at NAMEorg.org.

✦ The National Coalition Building Institute (NCBI) is an international organization that centers on leadership and training for diversity, equity, and inclusion issues in K–12 and university-level school settings. Find out more at NCBI.org.

+ The National Association of Independent Schools (NAIS) hosts an annual Diversity Leadership Institute. Find out more at tinyurl.com/ycld88m7.

+ Rosetta Eun Ryong Lee, a diversity consultant and teacher at Seattle Girls' School, has great resources on her website that center on cultural competence, diversity, equity, inclusion, and justice in classrooms and schools. Visit tinyurl.com/y9d2hhfz for resources.

Now it's time for you to think about your own inclusion practice.

# Stretching Exercise

## Self-Reflection

Take a few minutes to think deeply about your own possible assumptions and biases by answering these questions:

1. What cultural, social, or emotional biases do you have that might play a role in your teaching practice?

_____

_____

_____

_____

2. How might you monitor yourself so those biases are controlled when you interact with students?

_____

_____

_____

_____

_____

3. What ways could you integrate inclusive practices into your teaching so that *all* students can access the content?

_____

_____

_____

_____

# Doing More with Less

When you declutter your teaching, you have more space to focus on the things that matter most. Yes, there are so many shiny gadgets and flashy websites out there, but stay strong. Think before you buy a new tool or register for a new subscription service. Ask yourself, "What might be the purpose of this acquisition?" and "How might this help my students or my teaching practices?"

Even though there are so many educational technology resources and tools available, we need to resist the allure of the "latest and greatest" tech tools. Instead of being persuaded by shiny new things, we might like to think about doing more with what we already have, or doing more with less. For instance, instead of buying expensive robots and simply consuming them, we might prefer to create them from scratch with simple, everyday objects that we can hack. Simone Giertz's "useless" inventions (such as robots and gizmos that solve funny problems) are great examples of unleashing the potential of technology and showcasing the tinkering mindset.

Also, there's a lot that you can do with a limited budget. Even basic internet access opens a literal world of learning opportunities through activities and resources like online courses, classroom-to-classroom video conferencing, national organizations, virtual simulations…. The list goes on and on.

If we truly embrace the *tinkering mindset*—the mental process of creation and iteration—we could make bots with discarded electronics and recycled materials rather than buying a ready-made robot. Instead of seeing lack of budget or resources as a problem, we should see them as creative constraints, because "constraints can spur creativity and incite action, as long as you have the confidence to embrace them" (Kelley & Kelley, 2013, p. 126). Constraints and challenges force us to focus on what matters—the core of our inventivity or wit (our magical powers)—which turn us into active and daring learners who are persistent, flexible, and open minded. They also create the conditions for innovation; when we don't have what we think we need, we create it. And often, in the process of creating, we develop something that fits our needs even better. Limited resources force creativity, making the process more sustainable!

The consequences of becoming a digital minimalist might actually be soothing. Indeed, let's not allow technology to control us with its overwhelming nature; rather, let's regain our control by taming technology to serve our needs and aspirations. This allows us to focus on depth and to put pedagogy at the foreground. At the end of the day, the wow factor of cool new tools fades away quickly, but the strength and quality of the learning stays.

Though you might agree with these ideas in principle, let's take a minute to think about how we might do this in practice.

## Stretching Exercise

### Setting Goals

We believe that educators should always begin with the end in mind, not the tool. Inspired by Arthur L. Costa and Robert J. Garmston (2016), we can coach ourselves when planning: we first think about the potential learning outcomes, purpose, and goal; then we describe the success criteria that could be used to monitor and manage us as we teach. It's only in the final step that we should think about the possible resources that can support us in achieving our goal.

Practice these three steps for your next lesson:

1.  What is your goal / pedagogical objective / purpose?

_____

_____

_____

_____

2.  How will you know that you are successful (your criteria)?

_____

_____

_____

_____

_____

3.  What are some of the resources you might be able to draw upon (e.g., edtech tools, human resources)?

_____

_____

_____

_____

As you continue to monitor yourself as an ever-changing and ever-improving educator, you will become aware of strategies to activate, pause, and think deeply about your practice, but you might still be feeling unsure at times. Let's look at one more tip to continue this self-discovery and self-emergence!

# Building Confidence

Amy Cuddy's work on "power posing" has been transformational for many people. She explains how we sometimes feel like frauds, telling ourselves that "we are not supposed to be here." For instance, as a new teacher, you might question yourself when you have bad days, battling thoughts like "I am not supposed to be here," "I am failing," "I am never going to be a good teacher," and "Why am I not like so and so?" To these thoughts, Cuddy says, "Fake it until you make it!" Actually, she corrects herself and says, "Fake it until you *become* it!"

The idea behind power poses is that powerful body positions can actually make you feel more confident and less stressed. (You can find examples of these power poses online.) Cuddy suggests that you practice power poses for two minutes every day (or more, if needed!) and make this your routine. You can choose any power poses and practice them in the privacy of the elevator, the bathroom, or wherever you like! For more on the idea of presence and being authentic, watch the "How to Be Yourself in Conversation" Big Think interview by Cuddy (2016): youtu.be/YcGd5eBwQU4.

We believe that empowerment is not *given* to us but *comes out* of us. It's a choice, and it's *yours* to make!

# Understanding and Developing Awareness

This book has asked you to breathe, pause, and practice self-compassion. Now, let's continue being present with ourselves and strive toward becoming our best version.

As we close this chapter, let's return to Gattegno, who often talks about *awarenesses* in the plural, particularly within learning (Gattegno, 1987a, 1987b). Remember that one must first become aware of the opportunities for learning new things before one can be present to experiment and explore within the learning experience. Only through interacting with content, making mistakes, and trying new things can we truly become aware of what there is to learn. Then, with experience, we can make learning a more automatic process, requiring less attention/presence to activate new knowledge. The final level of awareness in learning is being able to transfer learned knowledge to new situations. Once we are aware of how to transfer past knowledge to new learning opportunities, we can activate this skill for the rest of our lives.

### Developing Awarenesses

In the next week, apply your learning from this chapter by taking a moment of self-reflection to write down your awarenesses every day. Here are some prompting questions for doing this:

✦ What do I see happening in the world around me? How do these happenings make me feel?

✦ How do I interact with my environment? With others?

✦ How do different environments, events, interactions, people, and settings make me feel?

**Awarenesses**

*(continued on next page)*

## Awarenesses

| | |
|---|---|
| **Day 4** | |
| **Day 5** | |
| **Day 6** | |
| **Day 7** | |

## *Inspiration*

### Being Bold

Here are some additional resources to further your learning of this new way of thinking and being:

✦ *Presence: Bringing Your Boldest Self to Your Biggest Challenges* by Amy Cuddy (New York: Back Bay Books, 2015): This book offers practical ways to become the empowered version of ourselves.

✦ *The Innovator's Mindset: Empower Learning, Unleash Talent, and Lead a Culture of Creativity* by George Couros (San Diego, CA: Dave Burgess Consulting, 2015): This is an excellent resource to empower yourself to take risks and start innovating in your own context.

# Share Your Vision

"The only way to find your voice is to use it."

—Austin Kleon, *Show Your Work!*

*I*n this chapter, we encourage you to envision ways you can share your practice with other educators who could be in the next classroom or around the world. You will explore the levels of connection in educations and see how you can build a network to better connect with others. Not only will this chapter be an exercise in self-reflection, but it will also act as a self-assessment to help you determine your level of interdependency. You will be asked to think about how collaborative you are, on both a local and global level.

## You Are Not Alone

Good news—you are not alone! Yes, you may be physically alone in your classroom when you are teaching; yes, you may be the only teacher stretching out of your comfort zone at your school; and yes, this loneliness may make you feel isolated, like you are the only one out there who embraces challenge, desires innovation, and looks for ways to expand your personal capacity. However, even though you might be alone in your classroom or school, you are not alone in your thinking. There are many other educators who feel the same way that you do. Those educators might be across the hall, down the street, or on the other side of the globe, but they *do* exist.

How do you find these like-minded educators? Understanding that you are alone is a good start but not enough. To find companionship and colleagues, you must put yourself out there. And you don't need to be an expert to share your practice. In a video about his book *Ditch That Textbook*, Matt Miller (2016) says, "Innovation is a skill. Develop it like a muscle." So allow yourself to go out there and share your work! Connecting with others makes you part of a broader professional learning community (PLC); and with the power of the web, your PLC can go beyond geographic boundaries. Just look at this book's authors, who live halfway around the world from each other and still wrote a book together! Many formal and informal opportunities exist for making these connections (something we'll discuss in detail in chapter nine).

## Being a "Glocal" Educator

There's a vast array of connections that you can achieve as an educator. Urie Bronfenbrenner's (1979) ecological systems theory helps us to frame connection levels within an educational setting. He identifies five levels within an ecological system (from narrow to broad): microsystem, exosystem, mesosystem, macrosystem, and chronosystem.

At the *microsystem* level, you can connect with other educators within your school. This might be a colleague next door or someone in a different department or grade level. Then you can broaden your connections to the *exosystem* level by connecting with other educators within your district or local school community. Educators at the *mesosystem* level think about how connections might occur across settings or systems. This might be educators collaborating between schools, or classrooms connecting with local community members on a real-world project. The *macrosystem* goes even broader; this could be other educators you meet through national conferences or professional organizations (like ISTE), or online through social media. Finally, a *chronosystem* looks at how connections change over time. Sometimes, you might work closely with educators in your school microsystem, while other times, you might collaborate or connect more with educators in your broader community.

Additionally, Jennifer Watling Neal and Zachary P. Neal (2013) introduced a networked model of the ecological systems theory that uses a student-centered approach to describe the complex connections that occur within educational systems.

Being a global collaborator is to have a sense of stretching yourself and looking at the big picture; however, we should also remember to take a look at the details, the parts, the tiny bits. It's important to be able to connect on multiple levels. The seventh ISTE Standard for Students—Global Collaborator—calls for students to "broaden their perspectives and enrich their learning by collaborating with others and working effectively in teams, locally and globally." Understanding the micro- and macrospheres with others is necessary to truly embrace global citizenship (Passeport, 2017). When we integrate the global and the local into the idea of "glocal," we become aware of the tensions and connections between the here and there. In this place where nothing is ever black and white, we can learn to thrive in grey, and have more space for critical thinking and depth.

In terms of technology, educator Manel Trenchs i Mola (art history teacher at Escola Pia Mataró in Barcelona, Spain) reminds us that "nowadays, our classes have no walls." While our students might seem isolated in a specific geographic area, we have opportunities to connect with other students or educators in locations that are far away from us synchronously or asynchronously. While we don't have equal access to high-speed internet, we can find creative ways to connect globally (e.g., by preparing our content offline and having one person responsible for sending the message later). In appendix B, you will find examples of glocal projects that connect students around the world.

## Who Am I in Relation to the Whole?

Holonomy, which derives from the Greek *holos*, meaning "whole," and the suffix *nomy*, meaning arrangements or distribution, is a systems approach that maintains that the success of an organization rests on the harmony and consistency between its parts (Costa & Kallick, 1995). The concept of holonomy can be used to understand complex organizations, like schools.

Schools are systems with structures and processes, for example, with a Board of Education; an administration; and policies, protocols, and procedures. By understanding how the different parts of education—students, teachers, culture, school systems, and leadership—work together, you can make decisions that are more beneficial to you and your students. Indeed, Richard Shavelson (1973) states that "the basic teaching skill is decision making" (p. 144).

As an educator, developing holonomy can be a powerful skill that embraces the two components of the ISTE Standards for Educators: being Learning Catalysts as well as Empowered Professionals. When we look at ourselves as agile designers of learning and creators of our own growth, we embody different perspectives, are able to see different points of view, and skillfully develop our craft. We are able to live and breathe our vision by making conscious decisions that align with our purpose.

There are many different systems that make up the school community as a whole. As educators, we are individuals who interact within those various school systems, as well as other systems outside of our school lives. For example, we are part a family (at home), a workspace, a sports team, a chess club. We constantly make decisions, consciously and unconsciously, on how to interact with the others who are part of this whole. When we develop holonomy, we become aware of ourselves and the impact we make on the whole, and then make decisions based on that knowledge. We understand that tiny changes and events *do* influence the whole. When one teacher is absent and needs you to substitute, you understand that tomorrow, you might be on the other side of the equation, needing a colleague to support you and cover your class. Another example involves the way in which you interact with your students. Do you know if your communication is having a positive or negative impact on them? Either way, this communication will impact their learning.

Holonomous teachers zoom in and out and act both independently and interdependently when they make decisions (Costa & Kallick, 1995). In schools, teachers make decisions all the time in the context of their classroom; however, they are not completely autonomous, as they need to represent and are influenced by the identity, values, and challenges of the school, district, and state, as well as the digital-age opportunities beyond that (social media, global collaboration, digital PLNs, etc).

Christopher M. Clark and Penelope L. Peterson (1986) summarize several research studies and report that teachers make about 0.5–0.7 decisions per minute during interactive teaching. Other interesting research findings were summarized by Robert J. Garmston and Bruce M. Wellman (2016): the more teachers collaborate, the more students learn! Therefore, educators need to be aware of their capability to go beyond ego by thinking about how the interconnectedness of their actions and the actions of others can influence school systems.

## Take a Breath

### The Systems We Are Part Of

As we look at how our personal and professional spheres create complex systems, let's take a moment to think about how they interact and influence one another. Think about some of the systems you are part of.

+ Microsystems (individual)—you might be a spouse, a father/mother, a gardener...

+ Exosystems (group)—you might be a skilled soccerball player on a local team, a churchgoer, a drummer in a band...

+ Mesosystems (district)—you might be a committee chair, a faculty representative, a department head, a member of the lower school team...

+ Macrosystems (national and global)—you might be a serial tweeter, a blogger, a YouTuber, an advocate of children's rights...

All of these parts make you a complex element of a complex system; so, as you begin to be more conscious about how tiny actions can impact the whole, strive to self-actualize by being deliberate as you align your mindset with your action set.

# Forming and Shaping Your Network

Michelle Cordy's keynote during the ISTE Conference in 2016 discussed how educators connect. In reference to Nicholas A. Christakis and James H. Fowler (2009), she shared the importance of forming and shaping our networks. As we think about these networks, we should consider the ways we connect with others and the ways others connect with us, directly or indirectly.

When we create networks, there is what Christakis and Fowler (2009) call a *topology*—a specific pattern that connects the dots. The table on the following page details three different patterns.

As digital-age educators and change agents, we need to develop diamond-shaped networks because, in doing so, we multiply bonds and create more interactions between different circles. It allows us to have a greater impact on the broader educational community—a ripple effect. The way people are bonded together through a structure can determine the impact they have on the whole. When the structure is linear, there isn't much collaborative scope; when we build a diamond network, however, we create a small world of diverse change agents driven by a specific goal, with all members contributing to a shared vision. Also, when we are more connected, we have more learning opportunities ourselves.

No matter the shape and scope of our network, we don't need to touch each individual and each network to make a difference; we can still impact larger systems through our actions within smaller networks. This also develops a sense of synchrony and harmony when we witness how our participation contributes to the creation of something bigger than us. You can determine the shape and scope of your own network by creating a mind map in the following stretching exercise.

| Unconnected | Bucket Brigade | Diamond Network |
|---|---|---|
| Unconnected individuals are all isolated from one another. | Bucket-brigade individuals connect linearly, to whoever is closest within their immediate environment. | Diamond-network individuals connect with people near them, away from them, and with those connected to their connections within the same network. |
| **Example:**<br><br>The teachers are isolated in their classrooms and are disinterested in collaborating. | **Example:**<br><br>The teachers from Grade 4 collaborate with the teachers in Grades 3 and 5 in their school. | **Example:**<br><br>Teachers from Grade 8 in school A collaborate with various teachers within their school and with teachers from school B. The teachers from school B collaborate with other teachers in their school and with teachers from school C. School C decides to collaborate with school A too. In this scenario, different educators within the school (at different levels), and from other schools or PLNs are interconnected. We visualize this as many networks whose connections originate and overlap in different places, both near and far. |

# Stretching Exercise

## Creating a Mind Map

Draw a mind map of your connections. Think about the people you collaborate with in your direct surroundings, then slowly move from the micro to the macro levels. What is the shape of your network—unconnected, bucket brigade, or diamond? Is it all of these? In which cases are you more connected and less connected? Try to get as complete a view as possible of your connections overall, both personal and professional.

Frequency of collaboration, when correlated with the levels of collaboration, is another way to demonstrate how connected you are. The next exercise will help you with this.

# Stretching Exercise

## Determining Your Frequency of Collaboration

Check or color the cells accordingly, to visualize the frequency of your collaborations.

| How often do you collaborate with . . . | Every day | Once a week | Once a month | Once a year | Never |
|---|---|---|---|---|---|
| teachers within the same grade level? | | | | | |
| teachers in another section of the school? | | | | | |
| a member of the school's leadership team? | | | | | |
| someone in another school? | | | | | |
| someone in your online global network? | | | | | |

Here are some additional suggestions for forming and shaping your network.

At the microsystem (individual) level:

+ Start a conversation with another educator at your school with whom you do not normally chat.

+ Spend some time walking the halls or working in a common space, like the library or teacher workroom.

+ With permission, observe other teachers' classrooms to get ideas for ways to collaborate.

+ Attend different grade-level or team meetings to learn what others in your school are doing. Think about ways that you might collaborate with them.

At the exosystem (community) level:

+ Attend local conferences or teacher meet-up groups.

+ Start your own meet-up group! Host a CoffeeEdu (CoffeeEdu.org) or other casual meeting for interested educators. Just don't have an agenda in mind—the only goal should be to connect with others.

At the macrosystem (global) level:

+ Attend national and/or international conferences.

+ Join professional organizations focused on edtech (CUE, ISTE and ISTE affiliates, etc.) or your subject area (NCTE, NSTA, etc.); and within those organizations, find ways to connect with others through special-interest groups.

+ Be active on social media! On Twitter, follow edtech-focused hashtags (Cybrary Man has a great resource page on Twitter chats at cybraryman.com/chats.html). You can join in the conversation, or just start by browsing the thread for ideas!

# *Meditation Prompt*

## Your Network

After examining the shape and scope of your network in the last few sections, what grabbed your attention regarding the importance of looking at different scales/levels?

_____

_____

_____

_____

_____

_____

_____

_____

_____

## *Inspiration*

### Being a Connected Educator

Here are some additional resources to further your learning of this new way of thinking and being:

✦ *Connected. The Amazing Power of Social Networks and How They Shape Our Lives* by Nicholas Christakis and James Fowler (New York: Harper Press, 2009): The authors will make you rethink how we see our relationships with others by digging into the many different types of networks we are part of or seek to engage in. This reading will allow you to broaden your horizons about networks, much beyond our educational circles.

✦ *The Global Educator: Leveraging Technology for Collaborative Learning & Teaching* by Julie Lindsay (Portland: ISTE, 2016): This resource will provide a way to deepen your understanding of global learning by engaging in an intercultural perspective. This book integrates the implementation of personalized learning.

# Open Journaling Space

# Open Journaling Space

---

---

---

---

---

---

---

---

---

---

---

---

---

---

# Open Journaling Space

_____

_____

_____

_____

_____

_____

_____

_____

_____

_____

_____

_____

_____

_____

# Open Journaling Space

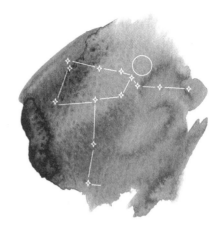

# Part 2
# Stretch

"If a human being dares to be bigger than the condition into which she or he was born, it means, so can you. And so you can try to stretch … stretch … stretch yourself."

—Maya Angelou

Yoga practitioners go through a series of poses, such as sun salutations, balance poses, inversions, and twists. Each pose stretches and strengthens different parts of the body. When you start a yoga practice, you recognize where your strong points are and where you need to strengthen. Sometimes, you even use props, or tools, to attain certain challenging poses or go deeper into others. With continuous practice, you become stronger and more flexible. Every time you step on the mat is an opportunity to grow and learn something about yourself.

The same thing is true for your learning practice. You may need to increase your flexibility as you balance your skill set, building upon your stronger areas as you strengthen the weaker ones. The goal is to stretch yourself in order to make yourself even stronger and even more flexible. In edtech yoga, we can consider technology tools as props to help us achieve our goals. Edtech yoga poses include different challenges that you may encounter as an educator, both in and out of the classroom.

Since you have reflected on how you might pause, breathe, and think in part 1, we will now share specific strategies for stretching yourself as an educator. The chapters in part 2 provide activities and best practices for taking action. Chapter four provides a plethora of suggestions for edtech integration, including tools in alignment with the ISTE Standards for Students. However, as you apply collaboration, critical thinking, creativity, and other digital-age skills to your teaching practice, you may encounter roadblocks along the way; chapter five discusses the importance of resilience and perseverance in face of these challenges, providing coping strategies. Then chapter six discusses the challenge of overstretching and the importance of balance as an educator, both in and out of the classroom.

# ISTE Standards for Educators That Connect to Part 2

## 3. CITIZEN

Educators inspire students to positively contribute to and responsibly participate in the digital world. Educators:

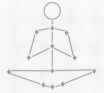

**3a**

Create experiences for learners to make positive, socially responsible contributions and exhibit empathetic behavior online that builds relationships and community.

**3b**

Establish a learning culture that promotes curiosity and critical examination of online resources and fosters digital literacy and media fluency.

**3c**

Mentor students in safe, legal, and ethical practices with digital tools and the protection of intellectual rights and property.

**3d**

Model and promote management of personal data and digital identity and protect student data privacy.

# 5. DESIGNER

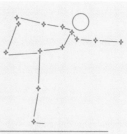

**Educators design authentic, learner-driven activities and environments that recognize and accommodate learner variability. Educators:**

**5a**

Use technology to create, adapt, and personalize learning experiences that foster independent learning and accommodate learner differences and needs.

**5b**

Design authentic learning activities that align with content area standards and use digital tools and resources to maximize active, deep learning.

**5c**

Explore and apply instructional design principles to create innovative digital-learning environments that engage and support learning.

# 6. FACILITATOR

**Educators facilitate learning with technology to support student achievement of the ISTE Standards for Students. Educators:**

**6a**

Foster a culture where students take ownership of their learning goals and outcomes in both independent and group settings.

**6c**

Create learning opportunities that challenge students to use a design process and computational thinking to innovate and solve problems.

**6b**

Manage the use of technology and student learning strategies in digital platforms, virtual environments, hands-on makerspaces, or in the field.

**6d**

Model and nurture creativity and creative expression to communicate ideas, knowledge, [and] connections.

# Tools Inside the Edtech Box

"It is not about the technology; it's about sharing knowledge and information, communicating efficiently, building learning communities, and creating a culture of professionalism in schools."

—Marion Ginopolis, "Digitaleading: Part II," *Big Think* blog

*T*his chapter provides a wealth of resources and tools for integrating edtech into teaching and learning. First, we talk about making learning visible and tangible. Because the digital world is intagible, it's not always easy to remember that student learning should remain at the center of everything we do. We need to keep the tech in the background and the pedagogy in the foreground. In other words, before we select tech tools, we need to ensure we know our pedagogical goal and what success will look like when we attain our objective.

Next, the chapter looks at edtech resources; we share how to curate and collect these resources for yourself so that you don't get overwhelmed. Then we share some of our favorite edtech tools and connect them to the ISTE Standards for Students. Though the tools are organized by standard, many tools can be applied to a variety of situations to help students meet multiple standards. Also, we talk about how you can adapt tools for your own purposes, because you know best what you and your students need. The chapter ends with edtech integration tips and tricks, including what to do when things go wrong, how to include students in classroom planning, a reminder of balance, and how you can contribute to the edtech community.

# How to Make Learning Tangible

Technology skeptics often argue that we are losing contact with the real world, while the digital omnivores adopt every new technology they can get their hands on. This book embraces neither of these scenarios. Instead of adopting an all-or-nothing philosophy, or taking sides, we would like for you to think mindfully about your use of technology. In every digital situation is an opportunity to decide how we might use the tool and why. We aim at focusing on those choices that we make along the way. So really, it's not so much about the technology; it's more about how we use it.

When it comes to technology, it's important to think about the ways in which we create an environment that is conducive to learning and the ways in which we respond to any unforeseen challenges that present themselves. As committed educators, we want our learners to understand, practice, apply, and transfer their learning.

Thanks to the myriad tech tools available to us, it is easy to create visible and tangible contexts for learning to occur. At the level of substitution, we can engage in many offline tasks and use digital tools (e.g., cameras, scanners) to capture reality. We can also go beyond merely capturing reality; with the use of augmented reality (AR) and virtual reality (VR) tools, we can offer students possibilities that were unimaginable a few years ago—and in infinite supply. For example, with AR tools, students can perform virtual dissections or explore the cells of the body. With VR tools, students can tour a museum, visit French-speaking countries, or even travel to the moon!

Just because so much is possible with digital tools and mobile devices, it does not mean that students should be glued to their screens. Instead, the devices should act as a means to an end. Yes, students should document their environment, but they should also learn to observe and interact with the outside world via their physical senses. Have students go on a nature discovery hike and use their device to take pictures of animal or plant species. Think about mobile devices as yoga props, like a block or a strap. The props are not meant to replace particular poses; they are meant to help you achieve something that would not otherwise be possible. Props help you to go deeper in your pose, deeper in your exploration journey.

# Selecting Resources for Your Toolbox

When you start looking for edtech tools to bring into your classroom, it might be difficult to know where to start. Technology is ubiquitous and ever changing; there are so many edtech tools out there that it is impossible to learn about every single one.

We also hear that we should think "outside the box"; however, in order to apply divergent thinking and appropriate our own way of integrating technology, we first need to know what is *inside* the box! A bit of conforming and understanding is required in the beginning so we can then adapt to our needs and wants, and find alternatives. As we slowly move into a zone that may be uncomfortable, it's reassuring to have a tools list; it provides us some relief and structure to not start from scratch. Curating is essential to selecting the right edtech tools for the right purpose. Here are some of our favorite places to find resources:

+ First, the human resource! Ask an edtech coach, your colleagues, or even your students as a first step.

+ The library! Your school's media center might already have great books about technology integration that are exactly what you are looking for.

+ Common Sense Media (commonsensemedia.org/guide/ essential-school-tools): This organization's site is *the* reference for digital citizenship. They have an entire section on edtech tools with many filters and reviews by parents and educators. You can also save and organize your edtech tools in collections.

+ Edtech Advisor (iste.org/membership/edtechadvisor): Free for ISTE members, this online resource offers a *huge* collection of edtech tools. And you can find what you are looking for by using filters to refine your search.

+ Focused online searches: Select the right keywords and make an Advanced Search on Google (google.com/advanced_search) to search for specific edtech tools.

+ Your PLCs (professional learning communities): As you network and find like-minded people, you create circles of people you can turn to when you need advice.

+ The tools you know: The best tools to hack are often the ones that are not only accessible but versatile in their creative options. A Google doc itself is a tool that can be unleashed for many purposes (to consume [reading, viewing], to create [making an ebook, hyperlinking, using as an interactive whiteboard], and so on).

Now it's time to take a look at our edtech tool lists, which align with specific ISTE Standards for Students. Our challenge to you: select one tool that you can try in the next three days!

# Edtech Tools to Enrich Your Practice

We have collected some edtech tools to give you a place to start in your edtech explorations. As noted earlier, these lists are organized by the ISTE Standards for Students, and each standard has a list of suggested tools that best align with that standard. That said, it's rare when only one standard is used in a lesson or project. Often, teachers will incorporate a variety of standards within the same lesson, thus integrating and blending together different practices. Also, students will call upon many of the standards as they create, design, and share their learning. So while the tools are organized by a single standard, they can be flexible too (just like you!). As you read, think about how each activity or tool might work in your classroom curriculum, as it will likely be used differently than it is in our examples.

Each resource table in this section includes the name of the tool with a link, a brief description, and a few ideas for classroom application. We do not include information about registration or pricing, because those are likely to change with time; however, many of these tools have free and premium options. Note, too, that some tools may require specific devices, but you may be able to adapt the resources and/or find alternative tools that work with your classroom.

*Caution*: Always be sure to check the copyright and privacy laws for tools before you sign up for them, especially before your students sign up for accounts. Different rules apply in different countries and for students of different ages. If you are in the United States, students under thirteen years of age are protected by COPPA (Children's Online Privacy Protection Act) privacy laws. For European users, ensure your school complies with the GDPR (General Data Protection Regulation 2016/679), which is a regulation on data protection and privacy for all individuals within the European Union. Also, be sure to check your school's privacy policies and technology usage rules before signing up for and using accounts.

## 1. Empowered Learner Standard

Students leverage technology to take an active role in choosing, achieving, and demonstrating competency in their learning goals, informed by the learning sciences.

+ **1a.** Students articulate and set personal learning goals, develop strategies leveraging technology to achieve them, and reflect on the learning process itself to improve learning outcomes.

+ **1b.** Students build networks and customize their learning environments in ways that support the learning process.

+ **1c.** Students use technology to seek feedback that informs and improves their practice, and to demonstrate their learning in a variety of ways.

+ **1d.** Students understand the fundamental concepts of technology operations, demonstrate the ability to choose, use and troubleshoot current technologies, and are able to transfer their knowledge to explore emerging technologies.

The empowered learner standard moves learners from engagement to empowerment. Technology has the potential to empower learners as creators and not just consumers of content. An empowered learner embodies the rest of the standards, because through technology, students take charge and gain ownership of their learning. An empowered learner has agency, develops goals, knows how to personalize his/her learning, and demonstrates learning transfer. Being an empowered learner requires enacting a growth mindset. The teacher acts as a guide to facilitate empowerment but does not take control of students' individual learning journeys; learning is ultimately for the student to experience. The physical classroom can also encourage student empowerment through design-thinking materials, flexible seating, learning zones, and opportunities to share student work.

Good tools to meet this standard are ones that allow students to create a reflective blog (1a), connect with a global audience via Twitter to enrich their learning (1b), gather feedback from one another via Poll Everywhere (1c), and develop Future Ready projects such as creating a tech support cell at school (1d).

## Empowered Learner Resources

| Tool | Brief Description | Classroom Idea |
|---|---|---|
| **Blogger** Blogger.com | A resource for creating and publishing a blog (an online journal) | Create and publish a school journal online. |
| **Poll Everywhere** PollEverywhere.com | A live, interactive online polling service | Conduct a quick vote in class and gather feedback. |
| **Socrative** Socrative.com | A tool for creating back-channel chats and live quizzes | Compare and contrast students' perspectives on an issue. Create choices/opinions on an issue and determine the top choices based on a democratic vote. |

## Empowered Learner Resources

| Tool | Brief Description | Classroom Idea |
|------|------------------|----------------|
| **Twitter** Twitter.com | A social-media tool with which users interact via short messages | Connect with experts of other classrooms to collaborate by searching for specific hashtags and handles, or by contributing with a class Twitter account (with a teacher's moderation). |
| **Seesaw** Seesaw.me | An online e-portfolio | Showcase student work and their learning processes. |
| **Future Ready Schools** FutureReady.org | Projects that empower students and personalize their learning | Create a student-led tech-support team in your school to troubleshoot tech issues and develop students' leadership skills. |

## 2. Digital Citizen Standard

Students recognize the rights, responsibilities, and opportunities of living, learning, and working in an interconnected digital world, and they act and model in ways that are safe, legal, and ethical.

+ **2a.** Students cultivate and manage their digital identity and reputation, and are aware of the permanence of their actions in the digital world.

+ **2b.** Students engage in positive, safe, legal, and ethical behavior when using technology, including social interactions online or when using networked devices.

+ **2c.** Students demonstrate an understanding of and respect for the rights and obligations of using and sharing intellectual property.

✦ **2d.** Students manage their personal data to maintain digital privacy and security and are aware of data-collection technology used to track their navigation online.

Part of life in the digital age is consuming and creating content as well as interacting within a global community. With a global community comes new opportunities but also new responsibilities for individuals. Therefore, it is imperative that students (and teachers) learn how to interact within both a global community and an interconnected digital world. Students need to think critically when they research, curate, reuse, and create with digital media as they build their digital footprint. The classroom can provide a safe space for students to learn about and practice responsible digital citizenship. The teacher can be a guide for students, facilitating opportunities for students to develop their digital citizenship skills. In addition to the tool list, we have created two lesson plans on digital literacy and digital citizenship. You can find links to these lesson plans in appendix C.

Tools that might help students meet this standard include the student e-portfolio GoEnnounce (2a), collaborating and reflecting through Google Hangouts (2b), content-search sites that alert students to intellectual property rights and responsibilities (2c), and extensions such as AdBlock Plus to block advertisements (2d).

## Digital Citizen Resources

| Tool | Brief Description | Classroom Idea |
|---|---|---|
| **Common Sense Media** CommonSenseMedia.org | A complete digital citizenship curriculum, including research findings about edtech, advice for parents, teaching resources, and reviews of edtech tools | Use the lesson plans on digital citizenship in your classroom. |

## Digital Citizen Resources

| Tool | Brief Description | Classroom Idea |
|------|------------------|----------------|
| **Turnitin**<br>Turnitin.com | An online service dedicated to preventing plagiarism and developing writing skills through personalized feedback | Have students use this service to check their work for originality and possible plagiarism to develop their essential referencing skills. |
| **Creative Commons**<br>CreativeCommons.org | A tool for searching and filtering creative content for media consumers or reusers, as well as a tool for generating a license as a creator | Use this website to teach about ways to find content as well as the best ways for students to protect and share their content. (This is where the learning happens about intellectual-property rights and responsibilities.) |
| **Adblock Plus (ABP)**<br>AdblockPlus.org | An extension that blocks advertisements on the Chrome browser | Simply ask your IT administrator to push this extension to all users at your school if you have G Suite for Education. |
| **GoEnnounce**<br>GoEnnounce.com | A site for students to develop a digital presence by learning about their digital footprint and how they can use digital media to showcase their achievements and creativity | Have students use this site to develop a digital portfolio, gain awareness of the importance of a positive digital image, and learn how to interact constructively and safely online. |
| **Google Hangouts**<br>hangouts.google.com | A chat tool with features such as video calling and screen sharing | Students can have real-time chats with their teacher and classmates while monitoring themselves on the way they interact with one another. |

*(continued on next page)*

# Digital Citizen Resources

| Tool | Brief Description | Classroom Idea |
|---|---|---|
| **Google Advanced Image Search** Google.com/advanced_image_search | A detailed filter for searching images, including specifics like text, color, aspect ratio, format, and usage rights | Have students search for reusable digital content with a usage-rights filter that allows them to use, share, and modify the content noncommercially. |
| **Pics4Learning** Pics4Learning.com | A free public-domain content provider intended for educational purposes | Use this safe space to look for copyright-friendly images for your classroom, student projects, videos, and more. The themes of the images mostly relate to elementary and lower middle school students. |
| **Photos for Class** PhotosforClass.com | A search tool that quickly locates Creative Commons images that are curated for students | Secondary school students can search for age appropriate, copyright-free images, and automatically cited images to use in a project while paying close attention to academic integrity. |
| **Pexels** Pexels.com  **Pixabay** Pixabay.com | Sources for public-domain images that are mostly conceptual and attractive for presentations | Find copyright-free images on these excellent websites, but be aware that some content needs filtering. |
| **Free Music Archive** FreeMusicArchive.org | A bank of free music and sounds that have a Creative Commons license or are in the public domain | Search by length, genre, and license, and download music for your classroom and student projects. |

## Digital Citizen Resources

| Tool | Brief Description | Classroom Idea |
|---|---|---|
| **SoundCloud** SoundCloud.com | An extensive platform for sharing sounds, music, and recordings with various licenses (copyrighted, Creative Commons, public domain) | Upload your music work or a creative recording (up to 5GB) and share it via a link. This is an excellent tool for developing authorship knowledge about musical creations. |
| **Free Loops** Free-Loops.com | A bank of instrument sounds that can be reused for music projects | Reuse these sounds to enhance music creations or for special effects in a performance or a video. |
| **SoundsCrate** SoundsCrate.com | A unique collection of public-domain sound enhancements, including sound effects, music, and sound design | This service is great for your interactive projects. Find and reuse a jingle as part of an advertisement creation or a flashnews sound for a video project on news literacy. |
| **SoundBible** SoundBible.com | A source for free sound clips and effects | Reuse sound effects for green-screen video projects. |
| **Dig ccMixter** Dig.ccMixter.org | An online bank of music that can be uploaded, remixed, and exchanged (includes music for commercial reuse) | Remix and reuse music for a video project, or lead students in a project to create and upload their own original music. |
| **Freesound** Freesound.org | A sound resource for uploading, sharing, and reusing sound creations (under different licenses) | Contribute to sharing globally by uploading a sound you created in your music class. |

*(continued on next page)*

## Digital Citizen Resources

| Tool | Brief Description | Classroom Idea |
|---|---|---|
| **Slides Carnival** SlidesCarnival.com | A collection of beautiful Google Slides and Power-Point templates | Use the templates to study the importance of design elements when communicating, then reuse the templates to present your own content. |
| **Openclipart** Openclipart.org | A completely free, public-domain clipart resource that allows reuse without providing credits | Have students find and include public-domain clipart in their presentations. |

# 3. Knowledge Constructor Standard

Students critically curate a variety of resources using digital tools to construct knowledge, produce creative artifacts, and make meaningful learning experiences for themselves and others.

+ **3a.** Students plan and employ effective research strategies to locate information and other resources for their intellectual or creative pursuits.

+ **3b.** Students evaluate the accuracy, perspective, credibility, and relevance of information, media, data, [and] other resources.

+ **3c.** Students curate information from digital resources using a variety of tools and methods to create collections of artifacts that demonstrate meaningful connections or conclusions.

+ **3d.** Students build knowledge by actively exploring real-world issues and problems, developing ideas and theories, and pursuing answers and solutions.

This standard aligns well with our postconstructivist philosophy (see chapter two) that knowledge must be created and discovered. Learning is a personal experience that requires individuals to make meaning. Thus, a knowledge constructor is a student who can effectively use technology to create knowledge.

In the following resource list, we focus on the ways that students can build knowledge through formative and summative assessments, particularly with video- and game-creation tools that can be used for review or testing. But there are plenty of other types of tools that can help students meet this standard, including finding information by using specific search engines like WebPath Express (3a), refining their media literacy skills via fact checkers like Snopes (3b), curating resources using Pearltrees (3c), or showcasing their problem-solving skills via Padlet (3d).

## Knowledge Constructor Resources

| Tool | Brief Description | Classroom Idea |
| --- | --- | --- |
| **Padlet**<br>Padlet.com | A digital, web-based bulletin board | Use for problem-based learning to show the process of constructing learning and solving problems step by step. (Posts can be moderated, password protected, or anonymous.) |
| **WebPath Express**<br>WebPathExpress.com | A search tool with multiple filters (reading lexile, language, age, etc.) within sites that have been checked for relevance and reliability by educators | Encourage students to research on Webpath Express first before doing a Google search. |
| **Pearltrees**<br>Pearltrees.com | A virtual organizer that offers visual coordination, collaboration, and sharing of resources | Initiate a Pearltree collaboration to brainstorm resources for a unit, with students actively contributing their ideas and resources. |

*(continued on next page)*

# Knowledge Constructor Resources

| Tool | Brief Description | Classroom Idea |
|------|------------------|----------------|
| **Flipgrid**<br>Flipgrid.com | A resource with which students capture short videos to share ideas and experiences with their classmates | Ask students to respond to a prompt via a selfie video recording. All student clips then appear in a channel. This is a way to experience vlogging and develop reflective skills and speaking skills. |
| **Formative**<br>GoFormative.com | An assessment tool that supports live feedback and includes a drawing feature | Use Formative as an online quiz tool that has the added value of a drawing tool. Ask students to develop or show their understanding of a concept by drawing from scratch or drawing on top of a picture or given background image. |
| **Kahoot!**<br>Kahoot.com | A game-based learning and trivia platform that is conducted live | Use existing games or create your own to help students review topics. |
| **Quizalize**<br>Quizalize.com | A game-based learning and trivia platform similar to Kahoot! that can be opened and completed at home | Personalize learning by tracking student advancement, and provide extra support or extension. This is the perfect tool for individualized learning plans. |
| **Quizizz**<br>Quizizz.com | A source of self-paced quizzes with automatic grading | Try "Live Game" for in-class participation or "Homework Mode" for content review on an individual level. |

## Knowledge Constructor Resources

| Tool | Brief Description | Classroom Idea |
|---|---|---|
| **Quizlet** Quizlet.com | A multiuse, interactive review tool that features flashcards, games, and more, as well as the option to create your own | Ask students to create Quizlet flashcard sets that they can use with each other in class as a review and demonstration of knowledge. |
| **Snopes** Snopes.com | A fact-checking site that researches and reports the accuracy of news, folklore, myths, and rumors | Students can check facts and contribute to the site, asking questions to develop critical-thinking skills. |
| **Plickers** Plickers.com | A data-collection resource that offers quick, formative assessments without requiring students to use technology | Use your smartphone as a quick assessment tool by asking students questions and then scanning their answers with the device. Students respond by holding up premade (scannable) cards rather than responding with technology. |

# 4. Innovative Designer Standard

Students use a variety of technologies within a design process to identify and solve problems by creating new, useful, or imaginative solutions.

✦ **4a.** Students know and use a deliberate design process for generating ideas, testing theories, creating innovative artifacts, or solving authentic problems.

✦ **4b.** Students select and use digital tools to plan and manage a design process that considers design constraints and calculated risks.

◆ **4c.** Students develop, test, and refine prototypes as part of a cyclical design process.

◆ **4d.** Students exhibit a tolerance for ambiguity, perseverance, and the capacity to work with open-ended problems.

The teacher shouldn't be the sole designer of what happens in the class-room. We can empower learners to be innovative designers not just in what they do in the classroom but in what happens in the classroom itself. We can engage students by asking them to be a part of curriculum planning by helping to co-design learning engagements and assessments, share ideas and resources, and participate in end-of-unit reflection. The classroom itself becomes a design cycle, where students and teachers both take a cyclical learning journey.

Think about innovative design as both a curricular choice and a way to provide students with agency—with choice, voice, and ownership over their learning. The teacher then becomes a facilitator or guide for the learning process, and the classroom learning experience becomes a partnership between students and teachers—a journey that we all get to experience and take together.

Some of the tools that we've selected for this list were once only available to professionals but have now been adapted for the classroom. These include video editing software, laser cutters (4a), AR (augmented reality) apps to plan and adjust a design before 3D printing (e.g., Object Viewer for MERGE Cube) (4b), printing design and modeling software (4b, 4c), 3D printers (4c), and creative and reflective tools such as Screencast-O-Matic that allow students to share problems about a project's process and persevere (4d).

## Innovative Designer Resources

| Tool | Brief Description | Classroom Idea |
|------|-------------------|----------------|
| **Object Viewer, a MERGE Cube app** mergevr.com/cube | An augmented reality (AR) and VR (virtual reality) app that allows users to upload and view 3D objects | This is ideal if you do not have a 3D printer or want to visualize your 3D design before printing. You just need a MERGE Cube (which you can make for free) to visualize your uploaded design. |
| **Screencast-O-Matic** Screencast-O-Matic .com | A screen and webcam recorder to capture and share video from your computer screen | Students can do screencasts to record their progress with a design project, reflecting and iterating along the way to improve their finished product. |
| **MakerBot** MakerBot.com **CraftBot** craftunique.com/ craftbot | 3D printers that make physical objects from a digital file by laying down multiple layers of some type of filament | Have students design and print something that they are learning about in class (e.g., the brain, geometric shapes, symbols from a book). MakerBot Education (makerbot .com/education/) provides existing designs and lesson plans to get students started. |
| **Tinkercad** Tinkercad.com | Free 3D-design software that can be used to build, create, and manipulate 3D objects virtually (onscreen) and physically (with 3D printers, laser cutters, or LEGO® blocks) | Have students design 3D objects in Tinkercad virtually, then create screencasts to share their designs. (This is a good alternative if you don't have the budget for a 3D printer.) |

*(continued on next page)*

## Innovative Designer Resources

| Tool | Brief Description | Classroom Idea |
|------|------------------|----------------|
| **Epilog Laser** EpilogLaser.com | A machine that uses a carbon-dioxide laser to cut or engrave different types of materials (e.g., acrylic, cardboard, leather, wood) | Art students can laser-cut print-making blocks; math students can learn about 2D and 3D visualization by making flat (2D) patterns out of cardboard and putting them together (3D); and social studies students can make "artifacts" for a museum. This is an expensive machine, but it's worth the investment—a versatile tool that can be used in any subject with any grade level! |
| **SketchUp for Schools** sketchup.com/ education/ sketchup-for-schools | Free, web-based 3D modeling software integrated with Google Drive and Google Classroom | Provide students with a file of virtual materials from which they can build their own bridge, housing structure, etc. |
| **iMovie** Apple.com/iMovie **WeVideo** WeVideo.com | Software to create, edit, and publish your own movies (iMovie is an app and software program, but it only works on Apple devices.) (WeVideo is a web-based program for collaborative video editing.) | Allow students to work individually or in groups to create a video on a particular topic of interest. |

# 5. Computational Thinker Standard

Students develop and employ strategies for understanding and solving problems in ways that leverage the power of technological methods to develop and test solutions.

✦ **5a.** Students formulate problem definitions suited for technology-assisted methods such as data analysis, abstract models, and algorithmic thinking in exploring and finding solutions.

✦ **5b.** Students collect data or identify relevant data sets, use digital tools to analyze [the data sets], and represent [the] data in various ways to facilitate problem-solving and decision-making.

✦ **5c.** Students break problems into component parts, extract key information, and develop descriptive models to understand complex systems [and] facilitate problem-solving.

✦ **5d.** Students understand how automation works and use algorithmic thinking to develop a sequence of steps to create and test automated solutions.

The computational thinker is a student who can use technology tools to analyze and manipulate data sets in order to solve problems. Students then use data and information learned from analyzing the original data to make connections to real-world circumstances. Computational thinking integrates STEAM (science, technology, engineering, art, and math) but can be applied to other subjects and scenarios (e.g., in projects where students design surveys, analyze the data, and present their findings).

Tools that can help students meet this standard include word-cloud generators to observe qualitative data (5a), data-collection tools such as Google Forms (which utilizes Google Sheets for its analysis) (5b), robots that require step-by-step assembly (5c), and tools that teach students coding by immersing them in situations where they have to break down a given problem into blocks or code (5d).

# Computational Thinker Resources

| Tool | Brief Description | Classroom Idea |
|------|------------------|----------------|
| **Bee-Bot / Blue-Bot** Bee-Bot.us **Cozmo** anki.com/en-us/cozmo **Ozobots** Ozobot.com **Sphero** Sphero.com | Robots specially designed for use in the classroom (Bee-Bot and Blue-Bot work well with younger children.) (Cozmo is a lifelike robot with a personality! Cozmo can be scaled up or down in complexity to be used with elementary through college-aged students.) (Ozobots are miniature, programmable robots that move along a track. Appropriate for primary years and up.) (Sphero is an app-controlled robotic sphere. Appropriate for elementary students and up.) | Teach younger students skills like directionality, estimation, and problem-solving with Bee-Bot/Blue-Bot. Students teach Cozmo new tricks through programming (from block-based to more advanced programming languages). Students use programming to create mazes for Ozobots to solve. With Sphero, students learn basic programming through collaborative, game-based STEAM activities. |
| **Google Forms** Google.com/forms/about **Google Sheets** Google.com/sheets/about | A free, G Suite tool that allows users to create and share surveys with a variety of response options A free, G suite tool that allows users to analyze data similar to Microsoft Excel or Apple's Numbers) | Ask students to come up with a problem around which they can design a survey to poll their classmates. Then have students use Google Sheets to analyze the survey results, identify potential solutions to their problem, and present their findings. |

## Computational Thinker Resources

| Tool | Brief Description | Classroom Idea |
|---|---|---|
| **Kodable**<br>Kodable.com<br><br>**Daisy the Dinosaur**<br>(available in Apple's App Store) tinyurl<br>.com/l29aju9 | Tools that teach coding skills to beginning or younger students | Have students play the games on Kodable in order to learn skills such as estimating, learning by doing, counting, and following directions.<br><br>Use Daisy to teach programming basics. |
| **WordClouds.com**<br>WordClouds.com | A free online service for generating word clouds using suggested words or a user-generated word list (similar to Wordle) | Students can use the open-ended answers from a survey to generate word clouds that identify the survey's main/recurring ideas and concepts and analyze the results further. The customizing options offer further opportunities to be creative (using shapes and colors for the word clouds). |
| **Scratch**<br>Scratch.MIT.edu | A highly recommended block-based programming tool for making interactive animations, stories, and games (created by the Life-long Kindergarten Group at the MIT Media Lab) | Ask students to create a game in order to learn about any subject. This very versatile tool can be integrated in any class! |
| **Chibitronics**<br>Chibitronics.com | A source for circuit stickers and other tools for making paper-based circuits | Combine arts and crafts with circuit building and programming—a perfect STEAM activity! |
| **Arduino**<br>Arduino.cc | Microcontroller board used to create interactive projects | Solve problems by tinkering with Arduino. Popular projects include developing an irrigation system with sensors or an alarm system for houses. Arduino allows users to build solutions and code to adapt to their needs. |

*(continued on next page)*

# Computational Thinker Resources

| Tool | Brief Description | Classroom Idea |
|------|-------------------|----------------|
| **Raspberry Pi Foundation** RaspberryPi.org | A computer that allows users to understand programming. Use the Raspberry Pi (with an SD card) along with a monitor, mouse, and keyboard. | Build your own weather station to collect climate data and explore data such as humidity, temperature, and air quality. |
| **Code.org** Code.org/learn **Codecademy** codecademy.com/ hour-of-code **Made with Code** (by Google) madewithcode .com/projects **Raspberry Pi Foundation** raspberrypi.org/ hour-of-code **Hello Processing!** (by the Processing Foundation) Hello.Processing.org **Khan Academy** khanacademy.org/ hourofcode **Tynker** tynker.com/hour-of-code **Udemy** tinyurl.com/ y84hjmlw | Different web-based activities designed to be completed in one lesson by beginners in alignment with the Hour of Code global initiative (started by Code.org) Some of the linked websites also have more advanced lessons and tutorials as students or teachers progress. | A great introduction to coding for anyone! Filter activities by topics, grade level, etc. |

# Computational Thinker Resources

| Tool | Brief Description | Classroom Idea |
|------|------------------|----------------|
| **littleBits** littleBits.com **Makey Makey** MakeyMakey.com **Snap Circuits** elenco.com/brand/snap-circuits/ **Squishy Circuits** SquishyCircuits.com | Creators of premade kits, parts, and activities designed to provide hands-on experience building circuits and other electronic devices (littleBits are electronic building kits that help students create and make inventions their own.) (Makey Makey works like a USB keyboard or mouse to create custom sensors for your computer.) (Snap Circuits feature premade pieces that "snap together" to make electrical circuits.) (Squishy Circuits use conductive and insulating playdough to make electrical circuits.) | Use electronic manipulatives to introduce students to the concepts of circuits and electrical engineering, allowing them to freely build, create, explore, and tinker! |
| **LEGO®** Education.Lego.com | LEGO® products that combine physical building and computer programming | Join a competition league to challenge students. Participating teams act as engineers and scientists to discover solutions to real-world problems. |

# 6. Creative Communicator Standard

Students communicate clearly and express themselves creatively for a variety of purposes using the platforms, tools, styles, formats, and digital media appropriate to their goals.

- ✦ **6a.** Students choose the appropriate platforms and tools for meeting the desired objectives of their creation or communication.

- ✦ **6b.** Students create original works or responsibly repurpose or remix digital resources into new creations.

- ✦ **6c.** Students communicate complex ideas clearly and effectively by creating or using a variety of digital objects such as visualizations, models, or simulations.

- ✦ **6d.** Students publish or present content that customizes the message and medium for their intended audiences.

The goal for this standard is creative and effective communication that demonstrates knowledge and learning. A creative communicator is someone who determines how they want to express their learning and takes advantage of communication tools to create their message. Rather than simply reproducing linear presentations of learned material, creative communicators develop original work in different modalities (audio, visual, tactile, kinesthetic), such as videos, podcasts, diagrams, models, simulations, cartoons, and books. Students consider their audience and learn the best ways to share their ideas with others.

Technology allows students to easily share their work beyond the classroom walls and thus develop a sense of audience and authorship. As creative communicators, students have the potential to make an impact on the broader community and world through the sharing of their knowledge, learning, and talents.

Tools that can assist students in becoming creative communicators include creative and interactive presentation tools, such as ThingLink (6a);

Edpuzzle, with which students can reuse, remix, and present information with interactivity (including questions for their audience, for instance) (6b); visualization and simulations tools, like Coach's Eye (6c); and video creation tools like YouTube Creator Studio, with integrated links, subtitles, and annotations that allow the audience to self-differentiate (6d).

## Creative Communicator Resources

| Tool | Brief Description | Classroom Idea |
|---|---|---|
| **Edpuzzle**<br>Edpuzzle.com | An app, website, and YouTube extension that allows teachers to make existing videos interactive with assessment questions | Pick a video and remix it (trim, pause to add a question, change the audio) to help students better understand a concept. |
| **Coach's Eye**<br>CoachsEye.com | A video analysis app that is popular in physical education but can be hacked for other situations that require close visual analysis and comparison | Students can videotape their movements and review them in slow motion. They can also compare two visuals and, therefore, improve their performance by practicing with intention and awareness. |
| **YouTube Creator Studio**<br>Studio.YouTube.com | A feature in YouTube that allows users to create a channel, organize and upload videos, and interact with viewers | Create a class YouTube channel to share student projects. (Remember to be a good digital citizen and check copyright and privacy rules before posting.) |
| **ThingLink**<br>ThingLink.com | A tool for creating annotated images and videos | Have students create an interactive map for their school, neighborhood, a country they are learning about, etc. |

*(continued on next page)*

## Creative Communicator Resources

| Tool | Brief Description | Classroom Idea |
|---|---|---|
| **Google Drawings** docs.google.com/ drawings | A web-based diagramming software that allows users to create charts, maps, and other visuals<br><br>(Available in the G Suite for Education) | Use this software to enhance lessons or have students create visuals to demonstrate what they've learned. |
| **Canva** Canva.com<br><br>**Easel.ly** Easel.ly<br><br>**Piktochart** Piktochart.com | Online templates and tools for generating engaging infographics (visual representations of data or information) | Students can use these tools to design posters for the student council, advertise for a fundraiser activity, or raise awareness about an issue. |
| **Book Creator** BookCreator.com<br><br>**Blurb** Blurb.com<br><br>**Storybird Studio** Storybird.com/ educators | Resources for writing, designing, and producing content in book form, both electronic (ebook) and printed<br><br>(Book Creator focuses on ebooks, which can include audio and video features, and is available as an iOS app or Chrome extension.)<br><br>(Blurb offers a platform for ebooks as well as print books and magazines.)<br><br>(Storybird also has a fund-raising program based on student creations, "from classroom to heirloom.") | Have students choose a topic to write a book about—perhaps for a younger grade or another class—then lead them through the production process, from content collection to the creation of the final product. |

## Creative Communicator Resources

| Tool | Brief Description | Classroom Idea |
|---|---|---|
| **StoryBoard That** StoryboardThat.com | A resource for digital story-telling through cartoons and storyboards | Create a comic strip to express or present an idea. (This tool is a particular favorite for language teachers.) |
| **SoundCloud** SoundCloud.com **Soundtrap EDU** Soundtrap.com/edu | Tools for making music or podcasts online | Create a classroom podcast that features students and teachers who post regularly about what they are learning. |
| **123apps Voice Recorder** Online-Voice -Recorder.com | A free and easy-to-use online voice recorder | Ask students to use this quick-and-easy tool for home-work assignments, like language practice, journal reflections, research tracking, etc. |

# 7. Global Collaborator Standard

Students use digital tools to broaden their perspectives and enrich their learning by collaborating with others and working effectively in teams, locally and globally.

+ **7a.** Students use digital tools to connect with learners from a variety of backgrounds and cultures, engaging with them in ways that broaden mutual understanding and learning.

+ **7b.** Students use collaborative technologies to work with others including peers, experts, [and] community members to examine issues and problems from multiple viewpoints.

+ **7c.** Students contribute constructively to project teams, assuming various roles and responsibilities to work effectively toward a common goal.

✦ **7d.** Students explore local and global issues, and use collaborative technologies to work with others to investigate solutions.

Some of the tools listed in the following table are for communication, because communication and planning are important parts of collaboration. In fact, *any* communication tools we include facilitate collaboration. But collaboration can look different, depending on who is involved. It can be real time or synchronous, and it can also be asynchronous, where participants collaborate on their own time when available. Global collaboration adds another layer of enhancement to student learning, allowing students to develop a broader perspective than they would otherwise be able to experience within the traditional classroom learning environment. Incorporating and interacting with a variety of diverse perspectives allows students to build upon and learn from each other to create something that is even greater than the sum of its parts.

To put this standard into practice, students can share their perspectives by creating digital content and sharing it globally (e.g., on 100 People) (7a); investigating issues with others and seeking different perspectives, as with PenPals Schools (7b); engaging in a Mystery Skype to develop problem-solving skills through specific roles and responsibilities (7c); and creating games that raise awareness about global issues with Games for Change (7d).

## Global Collaborator Resources

| Tool | Brief Description | Classroom Idea |
|------|------------------|----------------|
| **PenPal Schools** PenPalSchools.com | A project-based learning platform that connects students from around the world to "learn together" | Join a project as a classroom or with smaller groups to collaborate with other students internationally, seeking different perspectives and building empathy along the way (perhaps on a current issue such as immigration). |

# Global Collaborator Resources

| Tool | Brief Description | Classroom Idea |
|---|---|---|
| **Games for Change (G4C)**<br>GamesforChange.org | An online community that invites US middle and high school students to create digital games about the real-world issues impacting their communities | Students passionate about gaming can select a UN goal and create a game that raises awareness about it. They can also participate the annual G4C Student Challenge, a national competition held in the United States since 2015. |
| **100 People**<br>100People.org | An online, global initiative to foster mutual understanding, citizenship, and empathy while shedding light on global issues through 100 community-centric portraits at a time (stories, photos, videos, and other digital content) | Ask your students to create an authentic documentary about themselves or the people in the surrounding community that they then share on 100 People. |
| **G Suite for Education**<br>edu.google.com | Free data analysis, presentation, and word processing software through Google (mainly Google Docs, Sheets, and Slides) | Set up a project that students can collaborate on in real time. Have students write a collaborative story, or work on a lab report in class. The collaborative features can also be helpful for working with students outside of class or in other locations. For example, the brainstorming, outlining, and first drafts of this very book were completed in Google Docs! |

*(continued on next page)*

## Global Collaborator Resources

| Tool | Brief Description | Classroom Idea |
|---|---|---|
| **Google Hangouts**<br>hangouts.google.com<br><br>**Skype**<br>Skype.com<br><br>**Mystery Skype**<br>tinyurl.com/jfuwagy<br><br>**Slack**<br>Slack.com<br><br>**Voxer**<br>Voxer.com | Online tools for asynchronous and synchronous communication<br><br>(Mystery Skype allows students to solve a problem with other students around the world, assuming different roles while planning, executing, and reflecting on their experience.)<br><br>(Google Hangouts and Skype allow for audio and video communication.)<br><br>(Slack is a productivity tool that allows for different chat channels including audio, text, and multimedia chat options.)<br><br>(Voxer is an app and web-based communication tool that acts as a digital walkie talkie service, but allows for audio, images, and text communication.) | Use to set up, communicate, and work in teams. These tools can be good for cross-classroom collaboration, or collaboration among colleagues and professional networks. For example, the authors of this book are in an "edtech authors" Voxer channel. |

# Activities That Combine Student Standards

As mentioned previously, teachers often use multiple standards within the same lesson or activity, but what does that look like? This section provides two examples of classroom activities that blend together several standards. You will have an opportunity to try this out on your own as a stretching exercise that will walk you through the beginning steps for creating this type of activity.

**Example 1.** In this lesson, students participate in a Mystery Skype activity with another class. This activity combines three ISTE Standards for Students: innovative designer (4), knowledge constructor (3), and global collaborator (7).

**Innovative Designer**

Students organize themselves and use various tools to solve the challenge given to them: to find out where the other class is located by only asking yes and no questions. With Google Maps, they narrow down the mystery location; with Google Docs, they keep a record of the answers for verification.

**Global Collaborator**

Students collaborate with one another locally (in class) and globally (with the other class through Skype). They broaden their perspective by communication directly with the other class, and they assume different roles (investigators, researchers, record keepers, mappers, etc.) to achieve a common goal.

**Integrated Lesson**

**Knowledge Constructor**

Students use various tools to communicate and develop their research strategies. They think critically about the effectiveness of their collaborative skills within the class. After the lesson, they reflect on their strengths and areas of improvements.

**Example 2.** In this project, teams of students use the engineering design process to design, build, and test bridges. This activity combines the ISTE Standards for Students of computational thinker (5), creative communicator (6), and innovative designer (4).

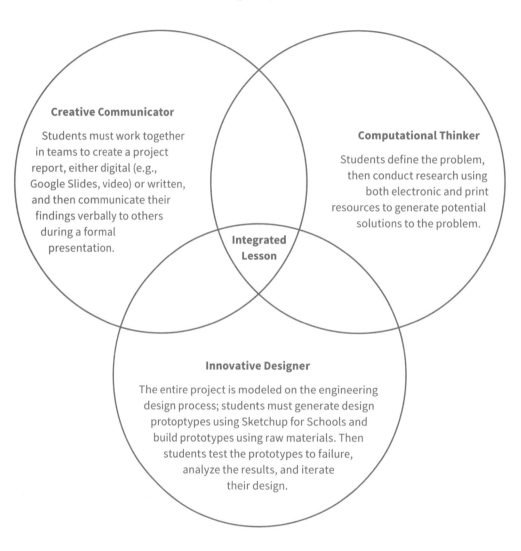

Creative Communicator

Students must work together in teams to create a project report, either digital (e.g., Google Slides, video) or written, and then communicate their findings verbally to others during a formal presentation.

Computational Thinker

Students define the problem, then conduct research using both electronic and print resources to generate potential solutions to the problem.

Integrated Lesson

Innovative Designer

The entire project is modeled on the engineering design process; students must generate design protoptypes using Sketchup for Schools and build prototypes using raw materials. Then students test the prototypes to failure, analyze the results, and iterate their design.

# Stretching Exercise

## Making Your Own Combined-Standards Lesson

Now that you have seen a few examples, it is time for you to create your own with this Google Doc:

noborderslearning.com/stretch-yourself

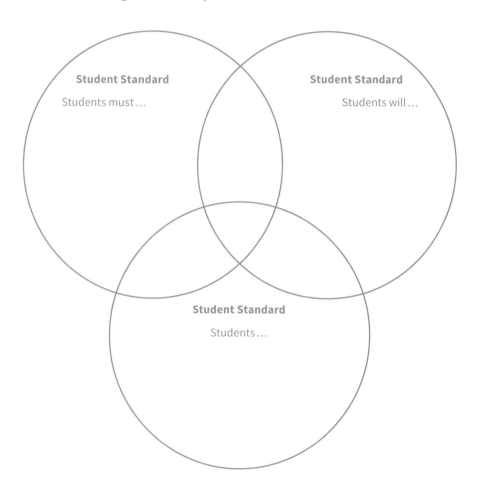

# *Meditation Prompt*

## Project Ideas

This chapter contains a multitude of tools for project ideas. Remember to pace yourself and stretch a little bit at a time, choosing one (or two) tools to try.

In the space below, think about some project ideas that occurred to you while reading this chapter. What purpose could some of the tools serve? What would you want to try first?

_____

_____

_____

_____

_____

_____

_____

_____

# Edtech Integration Tips and Tricks

Now that we have explored concrete ideas and suggested tools to use, we will share a few tips and tricks for successful edtech integration. These apply to any edtech tool that you might encounter in the classroom. As you experiment and explore, you might even come up with a tip or trick of your own!

## Have a plan B.

Just as you get ready to show that great video on the cell cycle, the Wi-Fi goes out. Or you walk into your classroom to share a new set of digital notes with students, and you spill a green smoothie on your laptop. Don't be taken by surprise when a technology snafu like this happens! Always be prepared for the unexpected by having a backup plan. Here are a couple plan B ideas:

- Plan a backup lesson that does not require you or the students to use technology. That way, when you lose internet access, your whole lesson is not derailed.

- Back up *everything* on the cloud. This can be Dropbox, Google Drive, or another cloud-based service. That way, if something happens to your device, your content can be accessed from anywhere.

Educator Renée Bogacz (instructional technology resource teacher at Channahon School District 17 in Channahon, Illinois) shares this with us: "When we use technology in our classroom, we shouldn't wonder what to do *if* it fails but should plan what to do *when* it fails, because it *will* fail sometimes; so we need to be ready to use that failure as an opportunity!"

Indeed, as much as you might anticipate problems, the key element here is to be able to make quick decisions when things don't go as planned. As we have learned, pausing and being present with the here and now is one way to find clarity when things get messy, so don't worry. If you keep your zen, you will find the resourcefulness you need to make mindful choices in real time. And even if your plan B doesn't work, there is always plan C, D,...all sorts of creative solutions!

## Ask your students to contribute.

Digital-age teaching and learning shouldn't be about being a "sage on the stage." It's true that you *are* the content expert who has the pedagogical knowledge, but that does not mean you cannot learn from your students too! Many students will have their own tech knowledge, expertise, and learning that they are eager to share; provide the space for them to contribute! Ask them to submit new ideas for learning engagements or assessments using a Google form or other surveying tool, or by contributing ideas on Post-it Notes on a dedicated board in the classroom. You could also have a weekly show-and-tell for tech tools, where students share a new or existing tool that they enjoy using.

Giving students a voice in the classroom helps them feel heard and valued, and it helps us, as educators, to grow our practice for authentic ideas to implement. Such habits create a stronger community, where all benefit.

## Space out new integration for best results.

Have you ever suffered from "app-list syndrome"? When you spend more time searching for tools than planning the actual learning outcomes of your lessons, you might need to pause and ask, "Why am I collecting gadgets?" When you realize that you are stretching too much by looking for too many tools and/or wanting to use them all, think back to part 1 by reminding yourself of your vision—your big picture.

While it's great to get really excited about technology, you also have to ensure balance in your usage. And what *you* experience might create a similar situation for your students too—perhaps they spend more time using the tech than actually learning through it. If that is the case, it's time to take a step back to reassess the situation. Spacing out your search of tools and their implementation is important; there's no need to try all the tools at once or to compete with colleagues about who is the most "techy" teacher. When all your actions revolve around student learning, you are on track. Like educator Angie Sutherland says, " The best app that exists is the thinking teacher."

*Inspiration*

## Teacher-led Technology Lessons

Here are some additional resources to further your learning of this new way of thinking and being:

✦ *Learning First, Technology Second: The Educator's Guide to Designing Authentic Lessons* by Liz Kolb (Portland, OR: International Society for Technology in Education, 2017): Using the Triple E Framework as a guide, this ISTE book talks about the intersection between best practices and choosing the right technology tools.

✦ *Creative Schools: The Grassroots Revolution That's Transforming Education* by Ken Robinson (New York, NY: Penguin, 2015): Sir Ken Robinson is a leading voice in education in the modern era. In this book, he describes transformative education methods to help students succeed in the digital age. Engaging and relatable, this book will help educators see the education system in a different light and think about how to use innovative teaching practices to revolutionize learning for all students.

# Tinkering, Failure, and Overcoming Fear

"Do or do not. There is no try."

—Yoda, *Star Wars: Episode V—The Empire Strikes Back*

Innovation is a process accomplished by connecting and building from ideas in order to solve problems. It's an iterative process, with designers in a constant loop of finding the problems, designing solutions to the problems, and then evaluating their solutions. And as educator Micah Shippee (social studies teacher at Liverpool Middle School in Liverpool, England) reminds us, "Innovativeness is the pedagogy for the future."

In chapter four, we introduced various tools that relate to the ISTE Standards for Students. In this chapter, we look at the tinkering mindset, stretching even further with the student standard of innovative designer. This standard aligns well with the designer and facilitator ISTE Standards for Teachers, prompting these questions: How can you, as a teacher, model stretching the standards? How can you design lessons that foster learning and learner empowerment by modeling stretching for your students? How can we use what exists to "hack the box" and model the ISTE Standards for Educators?

# The Tinkering Mindset

One way to embrace an iterative approach is to develop a tinkering mindset, but what exactly does this mean—to tinker? Merriam-Webster defines tinkering as working with things in "an unskilled or experimental manner." However, there is another way that we can view tinkering that sheds a more positive light. As Alec Foege (2013) argues in his book *The Tinkerers,* tinkering can be a disruptive act that takes existing materials and transforms them into something entirely new. He shows how the tinkering mindset generates some of the most innovative ideas throughout history, such as the US Postal Service and Apple computers. The tinkering mindset is about being proactive, courageous, daring, and confident. It requires creative confidence and the ability to fail forward (i.e., use failure to push yourself forward). The process of tinkering is also about rapid prototyping and being in the here and now. This means no more waiting and no more "thinking about trying." Embrace the unknown, the discomfort, the messiness of creativity! It is in the action that we transform.

# Thinking Outside the Box

There is no such thing as a perfect edtech tool—what works for one school or teacher may not work for another. Every tool has its quirks and every project/school/population/lesson is different. You need to find what works best for *you* and *your students.* Sometimes that means thinking outside the box. In chapter four, we gave you a toolbox containing some lesson ideas and technology resources that can be helpful as a starting point, though you may already have your own collection of resources. Now, we want you to reflect on how you can think *outside* the box.

For example, you can be agile in your use of edtech tools. Just because a tool is designed for a specific purpose does not mean you are limited to using it for that purpose only. Try out the tinkering mindset and "hack" tools to make them your own. Instead of starting from the beginning every time, take an existing lesson or tool and modify it to serve your purpose. Adaptation can be helpful in this situation. Do you want students to practice to reinforce a particular topic? Find an existing Kahoot or Quizlet set, copy it, and make it your own. Do not feel that you have to create your own—people share their resources and tools on the internet for a reason. They want you to adapt, modify, and share! Just be sure that you are giving proper credit when needed and that you are not copying anything that is protected under copyright. If you need help with this, refer to the "Edtech Tools to Enrich Your Practice" section in chapter four on digital citizenship. Even though that chapter focuses on students, many of the resources work for educators too.

## Edtech Integration in Action

The first step in technology integration is awareness of what tools are available, as we shared in chapter four. But once you are aware, how do you put your awareness into action? The next step is to implement edtech tools in the moment, when a need arises. Though this process may be challenging as you learn the best ways for you and your students to integrate new edtech tools, remember that the ultimate goal is to make edtech integration invisible. As technology is ubiquitous and versatile, it should flow and become a natural part of your lessons.

According to Sinek (2011), the WHAT is the result of our actions (the HOW) that are driven by our purpose (the WHY). When it comes to integrating edtech into your lessons, we recommend that you don't start with the tech tools. It's useful and reassuring to have lists of edtech tools and to have them aligned with the ISTE Standards; however, lists and tools are not useful by themselves. It's only when we integrate the tools into our pedagogy that they enhance or accelerate the learning of our students.

The following table shows practical, mini lesson plans that showcase deliberate teaching for deliberate learning, or how we can plan backward to meet the needs of the students. As educators, we observe our students and, in so doing, we know what they might require to learn their next lesson. As we identify students' needs, we can design the steps that generate learning, but we can also adjust and alter our plans to address unforeseen classroom needs. Use the stretching exercise after the table to explore some of your own deliberate-teaching-and-learning lesson plans.

Before we proceed, let's revisit the four phases of learning explained in chapter two:

+ Phase 1: Be aware that there is something new to be learned.
+ Phase 2: Explore through trial and error.
+ Phase 3: Practice until it's automatized.
+ Phase 4: Transfer to another learning situation.

Note: if your content is totally new to students, you might want to deliberately plan learning engagements that promote phases 1 and 2 in one lesson and then continue to phases 3 and 4 in another lesson (or two).

## Examples of "Deliberate Planning for Deliberate Learning"* Lesson Plans

| Deliberate-Planning Practice: Teacher Action | Deliberate-Learning Practice: Student Impact |
| --- | --- |
| 1. I want the students to learn . . . <br><br> 2. So my success criteria include . . . <br><br> 3. Therefore, I will need to . . . | 1. Students gain . . . <br><br> 2. ISTE Standards for Students that apply include . . . |
| **Teaching a Grammar Point in French** | |
| 1. I want the students to learn the difference between *une* and *la* in French. <br><br> 2. So my success criteria include: (a) students become aware that there are two concepts to learn, (b) students can apply the two concepts in different situations, and (c) students have the opportunity to transfer their understanding of the difference between *une* and *la* to *un* and *le*, where the gender changes from feminine to masculine. <br><br> 3. Therefore, I will need to (a) plan visible and tangible situations that trigger awarenesses (a demo using Cuisenaire™ rods), (b) get students to pay attention to the situation (observations to be recorded on Socrative), and (c) have students practice in pairs (to create the voiceover of a situation given on Seesaw) and alone (replace the word "rod" with something of their choice), and create three sentences on Google Classroom for the next class, along with an object they bring. | 1. Students gain valuable foreign-language practice and skills within a particular language and grammar point. <br><br> 2. ISTE Standards for Students that apply include: <br><br> ✦ Empowered Learner (1) <br> ✦ Knowledge Constructor (3) <br> ✦ Innovative Designer (4) <br> ✦ Creative Communicator (6) |

*(continued on next page)*

## Examples of "Deliberate Planning for Deliberate Learning"* Lesson Plans

| Deliberate-Planning Practice: Teacher Action | Deliberate-Learning Practice: Student Impact |
|---|---|
| 1. I want the students to learn . . . <br><br> 2. So my success criteria include . . . <br><br> 3. Therefore, I will need to . . . | 1. Students gain . . . <br><br> 2. ISTE Standards for Students that apply include . . . |
| **Teaching How to Identify "Fake News" in Digital Literacy** | |
| 1. I want the students to learn how to identify "fake news" and apply critical thinking when informing themselves and others. <br><br> 2. So my success criteria include: (a) students become aware that not everything online is true, (b) students realize that they need tools to analyze news, (c) students can create a fake-news video on a topic of their choice to demonstrate some of the components of fake news, and (d) students know how to review each others' news. <br><br> 3. Therefore, I will need to (a) understand students' prior knowledge, (b) provide space for students to research and inquire about what the components of fake news might be (the black-and-white and the grey areas), and (c) show students how to create a fake-news video and how to evaluate one another. <br><br>   ✦ GRASPS Assessment—Fake News: goo.gl/2RKsJT <br>   ✦ GRASPS Template: goo.gl/CJ6fro | 1. Students gain valuable digital-age skills, including critical thinking and information literacy. <br><br> 2. ISTE Standards for Students that apply include: <br><br>   ✦ Empowered Learner (1) <br>   ✦ Digital Citizen (2) <br>   ✦ Knowledge Constructor (3) <br>   ✦ Creative Communicator (6) <br>   ✦ Global Collaborator (7) |

## Examples of "Deliberate Planning for Deliberate Learning"*
## Lesson Plans

| Deliberate-Planning Practice: Teacher Action | Deliberate-Learning Practice: Student Impact |
|---|---|
| 1. I want the students to learn . . .<br><br>2. So my success criteria include . . .<br><br>3. Therefore, I will need to . . . | 1. Students gain . . .<br><br>2. ISTE Standards for Students that apply include . . . |
| **Teaching 2D-to-3D Visualization in Math** | |
| 1. I want the students to learn how to manipulate flat patterns (2D objects) to create 3D shapes.<br><br>2. So my success criteria include: (a) students can match a 2D shape with its 3D shape, (b) students can create a 2D flat-pattern design that they can successfully turn into a 3D shape.<br><br>3. Therefore, I will need to (a) understand students' prior knowledge and attitudes toward math, (b) provide exercises to help students develop their visualization skills, and (c) create a project that allows students to apply their learned knowledge in a constructive situation. | 1. Students gain valuable visualization skills for use in STEM subjects and real-world, problem-solving situations.<br><br>2. ISTE Standards for Students that apply include:<br>  ✦ Innovative Designer (4)<br>  ✦ Computational Thinker (5) |

*(continued on next page)*

## Examples of "Deliberate Planning for Deliberate Learning"* Lesson Plans

| Deliberate-Planning Practice: Teacher Action | Deliberate-Learning Practice: Student Impact |
|---|---|
| 1. I want the students to learn . . . <br><br> 2. So my success criteria include . . . <br><br> 3. Therefore, I will need to . . . | 1. Students gain . . . <br><br> 2. ISTE Standards for Students that apply include . . . |
| **Teaching Circuits in Science** | |
| 1. I want the students to learn the basics of circuits. <br><br> 2. So my success criteria include: (a) students can identify basic circuits, (b) students can tell the difference between an open and a closed circuit, (c) students understand how to construct a parallel circuit and a series circuit, and (d) students understand the purpose of using circuits. <br><br> 3. Therefore, I will need to (a) understand students' prior knowledge; (b) provide content knowledge related to the basics of circuits, including vocabulary; (c) introduce concepts of electrical engineering and its social impact; and (d) provide opportunities for students to explore concepts using tangible objects. | 1. Students gain knowledge and understanding of circuits and how to apply them to real-world situations. <br><br> 2. ISTE Standards for Students that apply include: <br><br> ✦ Knowledge Constructor (3) <br> ✦ Innovative Designer (4) <br> ✦ Computational Thinker (5) |

*The phrase "deliberate planning for deliberate learning" was coined by educator Daisy Rana.

# Stretching Exercise

## Deliberate Teaching for Deliberate Learning

Now that we have provided some examples of deliberate teaching for deliberate learning, it is time for you to think of some ideas from your classroom experience.

| Deliberate-Planning Practice: Teacher Action | Deliberate-Learning Practice: Student Impact |
|---|---|
| 1. I want the students to learn . . . <br><br> 2. So my success criteria include . . . <br><br> 3. Therefore, I will need . . . | 1. Students gain . . . <br><br> 2. ISTE Standards for Students that apply include . . . |

[Lesson Title]

| | |
|---|---|
| 1. _____ <br><br> 2. _____ <br><br> 3. _____ | 1. _____ <br><br> 2. _____ |

[Lesson Title]

| | |
|---|---|
| 1. _____ <br><br> 2. _____ <br><br> 3. _____ | 1. _____ <br><br> 2. _____ |

# The Importance of Failure

When you seek to be innovative, you will encounter failure—something many people fear—but failure *and* fear are important parts of the process of change. "How can fear be important to the process?" you ask. "Isn't it a *bad* thing to be afraid?" On the contrary! Change is hard *because* it's scary; fear is proof that you are trying something new and different—that change in on the horizon. Fear is a necessary phase of the growth process.

In her research, Carol Dweck (2015) defines the terms *fixed mindset* and *growth mindset*: A fixed mindset views intelligence and skill as innate with no chance for development. A growth mindset, however, views intelligence and skill as things to be developed through learning. Dweck says that a person with a growth mindset looks at failure by saying, "Mistakes are so interesting. Here's a wonderful mistake. Let's see what we can learn from it."

We all have fixed and growth mindsets in certain aspects of our lives. However, experiencing failure and learning how to fail gracefully give us opportunities to develop and work on reinforcing and supporting our growth mindset. Having a growth mindset does not mean that change is easy; it means that you are able to achieve *in spite of* the fear. So don't shy away from failure. As educator Jennifer Garner (@educatorjenn) says, "Accepting failure is a stage of growth. Learn from it and go on." We need to let failure be part of our learning journey, as we can only move on by bouncing back first.

Educators are encouraged to create learning situations that the students are *almost* able to do. This is a way to challenge students appropriately and adapt the teaching to the needs of students for deliberate learning. In these situations, the students will learn through a trial-and-error process. Gattegno (1977, p. 1) describes *mistakes* as "mis-takes" (which happen unintentionally when we "*take* something for what it is not") (emphasis added) and talks about *errors* as evidences of learning—evidence of being in the unknown and striving. The difference can be significant in the way we see learning: "Errors underline the matter with which we are linked; mistakes underline the person who is involved in the activities" (Gattegno, 1977, p. 1). Gattegno also says that errors are "gifts to the class" (Favre, 2015, p. 68).

Indeed, errors offer us the opportunity to try again, to try better, and to ultimately succeed.

Learning to fail can also teach grit. Researcher Duckworth (2013) says that "Grit is passion and perseverance for very long-term goals. Grit is having stamina." As educators, we want our students to develop passion for learning, perseverance when life is difficult, and the stamina to develop and attain long-term goals. These are skills that will not only be useful when learning in the classroom but also throughout life. Because, as we all know, failure is a part of life. It is inevitable no matter how hard we try to avoid it. What we can do, though, is work on how we react to failure when it occurs.

If we want to work on developing our learning-to-fail muscles, we need to try new things. We need to create opportunities for failure! Then we need to embrace failure with gratitude and an open mind. This is something that is important for us to model as educators so that we can guide our students toward developing these muscles in themselves.

We might also see the situation from a different perspective when we encounter failure. Educator Tania Driskill (from Bolivar High School in Bolivar, Missouri) shares her insight about how what we perceive as problems in our teaching can become learning gifts for our students: "When a lesson idea doesn't work, stay calm, nod, and feel glad this happened, because one important skill for the future, one that our students need to develop, is to effectively respond to crisis or problems."

# Stretching Exercise

## Creating a Bug List

Have you ever heard of a bug list? A bug list is an idea from Tom Kelley in *The Art of Innovation* (2013). It is a way to keep track of a list of things that bug you about the world. The point of this list is not to complain or get down on the world but to identify potential problems so that you can then develop potential solutions. Start your own bug list on the next page.

1. _____

2. _____

3. _____

4. _____

5. _____

6. _____

7. _____

8. _____

9. _____

10. _____

## Making Fear Your Friend

"What would you do if you weren't afraid?" asks Sheryl Sandberg (2013, p. 12) in her book *Lean In: Women, Work, and the Will to Lead*. Fear is a feeling that educators are often in contact with. Fear can be seen as a problem. In his fantastic children's book, *What Do You Do With an Idea?*, Kobi Yamada (2014) explains what to do with a problem: "Initially, we resist change, we are worried about it, [and] we ignore it or try to shoo it away; but it's only when we face and tackle problems that we find something beautiful in them: *opportunities*."

Educator Mark Reid (a Varkey Foundation teacher ambassador and the Looking@2020 project leader) shares his experience on making a friend of fear: "My professional life changed the moment I started saying 'yes!' to opportunities and challenges that once scared me. Knowing your skills and abilities as an educator must include knowing your worth and being willing to adapt or apply those skills to new experiences. I discovered a whole new realm of possibility for myself and for my students."

Like Reid, if we acknowledge fear and allow it to be an opportunity rather than a problem, it can motivate us! We can use it to our advantage to push through and stretch ourselves, but this comes with practice. In embracing the fear and learning to live with the discomfort of it, you will be able to stretch further than you ever could without it.

## Tackling Fear

Here are some tips for dealing with fear.

✦ Use breathing exercises. Try using the box breathing method to calm yourself. Breathe in four counts, hold the breath for four seconds, breathe out for four seconds, hold the breath for four seconds, repeat. This will calm your body and allow you to feel better about being in a "fearful" place. If breathing is not enough, try jumping up and down or some other physical movement. This might even be a good time to try a power pose (remember those from chapter two?).

✦ Be honest with your students. Tell them, "We are going to try something new today. It may go well or it may not, and not knowing the outcome can be a little scary. But it's all okay, because we are going to learn something either way!" Being open and transparent with your students builds a level of trust and understanding in your classroom. It also models to your students how to embrace fear as part of the learning process.

*(continued on next page)*

> ✦ Of course, the same classroom model on fear also applies to you: don't be afraid if things go wrong. As long as you have a backup plan, it will allay your fears—you won't be caught stuck in an awkward situation—and the lesson will go on. (You will learn something either way!)
>
> ✦ Make sure that you are balanced and centered. In the next chapter, we will go into more detail about how to practice balance to avoid stress—because if you are stressed, you will be more vulnerable to succumbing to your fears. You need to have a base level of health and mindfulness before thinking about stretching beyond.

Creativity takes time. This means that you may need to hang out with fear for a while before the creative juices start flowing. Pink (2010) says that in order to reach high levels of creativity, we need intrinsic motivation, which is defined as "the drive to do something because it is interesting, challenging, and absorbing" (p. 46). We all know the truth of the matter: even when you come up with a new idea, it might not work. So whenever you start the creative process, there will be a fear of failure, but your *drive* (your intrinsic motivation) can help you to overcome the disappointment when the process doesn't go according to your original plans.

Remember what you tell your students: it is okay to fail! And the more time you hang out with fear, the easier it will become to embrace it and stretch beyond your comfort zone. Use the following meditation prompt to reflect on the fear that might come for you with change, then work on changing your habits of comfort when it comes to this fear.

# Meditation Prompt

## Embracing Fear

Use this space to reflect on what you want to change in your teaching practice. Think about what your fears might be when it comes to making that change. What is holding you back or blocking your path? Consider how you could allay those fears—or embrace them! How could you turn your fears into an opportunity to learn and to grow?

## Learning to Create, Creating to Learn

Here are some additional resources to further your learning of this new way of thinking and being:

+ *Invent to Learn: Making, Tinkering, and Engineering in the Classroom* by Sylvia Libow Martinez and Gary Stager (Torrance, CA: Constructing Modern Knowledge Press, 2013): This book provides a clear explanation of how to bring the maker movement to your students, the active learners at the center of the classroom. With that in mind, the authors provide the what, how, and why of classroom makerspaces at *any* budget and level.

+ *Beautiful Oops!* by Barney Saltzberg (New York: Workman, 2013): This is a fun and colorful children's book that teaches all of us that it's okay to make mistakes!

# Caution: Don't Overstretch

"Sometimes, when we are beating ourselves up, we need to stop and say to that harassing voice inside, 'Man, I'm doing the very best I can right now.'"

—Brené Brown, *Rising Strong*

ow that we have covered a variety of strategies and tools for stretching yourself, we know that you might be excited to try it all right away—but *be careful*! Stretching yourself is a good thing, but we do not want you to overstretch. Overstretching is a real concern, particularly with eager educators who have the best of intentions. In this chapter, we stress the importance of keeping balance. We discuss how sometimes, less is more. We also discuss the importance of taking care of yourself. We want you to focus on the journey, not just the destination.

## How Much Is Too Much?

You want to do well. You want to succeed. You want to be a teacher rockstar. If you didn't, you wouldn't be reading this book! However, the drive for success can be draining. The threat of teacher burnout, especially as a new teacher, is real. Don't let this happen to you! Learn to recognize when you have had enough—when you are done. Remind yourself what your purpose and vision are, as you developed in part 1. There is no need for you to overdo it. Ambition is the drive to do; however, doing too much will impact the quality of your work.

Stephen Covey's book *The 7 Habits of Highly Effective People* tells you to pay attention to the skill of "sharpening the saw"—to balance your energy to be effective not in the now but sustainably (1989, p. 299). This means that you need to practice your breathing exercises, allowing yourself to pause and refocus your action with your intentions, your big WHY. What are some signs of imbalance and burnout? Watch your energy levels. If you feel tired all the time or groan every morning when you wake up, you might be on a path to burnout. Attitude is also a critical component. If you notice yourself complaining or using more negative talk—whether that negativity is internal or external—it might be another sign of burnout.

## Exploring Minimalism

While you might be ambitious and unstoppable, it's possible you could benefit from doing a bit less. Effective people focus on a few projects that they excel at, then they move on to other goals. For instance, you might be interested in mindfulness and revisiting your teaching philosophy. Maybe you wonder about applying a minimalist approach to edtech, such as having fewer tech tools and more pedagogical depth? Before you jump in with your planning, take a deep breath (part 1), sit back, and relax. Watch yourself from a distance and imagine the kind of educator you want to be. You might be surprised to realize just how much simplifying your practice allows you to focus on what matters the most: your students. So how do we become minimalist educators? By focusing on the learning. If you always focus on the learning goals and objectives *first*, then you can "unlock the power of student-centric learning with technology" (Dhingra, 2012).

## Balance—Less Is More

If you go too far on the side of technology, you might fall over. If you stretch too much, you might end up hurting yourself. Your intentions may be good, but contrary to popular belief, you *can* have too much of a good thing. If you keep adding, adding, adding, when do you stop to measure what you've achieved? What are you hoping to achieve? You might accomplish a packed scheduled, stressed students, or teacher burnout, none of which you want.

Best practices include introducing balance to your classroom—both for you and for your students.

One of the easiest imbalances to fall into is getting overwhelmed by trying to do too many new things all at once. We understand—you are a motivated teacher who wants to do more. When you are inspired, you may want to implement all of your ideas all at once, but this is impractical. You can't do everything all at once. But you *can* do one thing at a time. Don't try to boil the ocean; instead, start with a pot of water. Later, once you master the pot of water (or decide that pot of water isn't going to boil), you can try another. And another. (And so on.)

Use the following stretching exercise to practice narrowing your list of edtech ideas.

# Stretching Exercise

## Setting Goals: Twenty-Five to Five

Make a list of twenty-five edtech-related goals. These could be lessons that you want to try, new tools, project ideas, etc.

1. _____     7. _____

2. _____     8. _____

3. _____     9. _____

4. _____     10. _____

5. _____     11. _____

6. _____     12. _____

13. _____     20. _____

14. _____     21. _____

15. _____     22. _____

16. _____     23. _____

17. _____     24. _____

18. _____     25. _____

19. _____

Now that you have twenty-five goals, choose the top five from your list.

1. _____

2. _____

3. _____

4. _____

5. _____

According to businessman Warren Buffett, you should focus on achieving only those top five goals and forget the rest. You can come back to the larger list once you are ready to try more new things—but only after you accomplish your top five. The idea behind this exercise is to determine what is truly important to you and work on that above all else.

# Taking Care of Yourself

This chapter is not intended to alarm you; we just want you to remember to take care of yourself, first and foremost. One strategy for self-care is limiting the amount of time that you spend on stretching. Think about the recommendations for limiting screen time. All screens all day is not a good idea, and neither is constantly stretching yourself. Even the most eager technology users recognize the importance of considering screen time. You don't want to stretch all your muscles every day, as you might end up hurting yourself. So focus on stretch time in moderation, building your stretching muscles slowly. The first day of yoga is not the time to attempt a full handstand, and the first day at a new job or school is not the time to attempt a full transformation. Success occurs over time, as you practice, build up the foundational poses, and develop the necessary skills.

## *Meditation Prompt*

### Taking Care of Yourself

What are some ways that you might take care of yourself? How do you like to destress?

---

---

---

---

---

_____

_____

_____

_____

_____

_____

_____

_____

## Focusing On the Journey, Not Just the Destination

Knowing your ultimate destination can help you plan your path, but the end should be only part of the journey. There is value in the journey itself; what you experience and learn along the way can be just as effective as what you achieve in the end—and probably more so, especially when you consider the value of transferring one journey's lessons to the next. Think about the advice we give students: enjoy learning for learning's sake and not just the grade or test score. We, as educators, should take this same advice. Yes, it is good to have goals, but remember to enjoy and embrace the stretching journey itself.

Your stretching journey is just that—*yours*. Avoid comparing yourself to other educators; there will always be educators who are less and more flexible than you, just like there are varying levels of flexibility in yoga. Focus on your growth and progress, because it is your personal journey that matters most. Even within your own learning practice, it will be easier to stretch in certain areas than it is in others. Perhaps you are more comfortable stretching in the direction of hands-on activities, but you have trouble going beyond the safety of your classroom to create new opportunities for your students to communicate. Whatever the area is that you find harder to stretch, know that it is okay. It is normal to have varying flexibility—we *all* have unique strengths and weaknesses.

Focus on the journey. Embrace the experience and the daily challenges of your stretching practice. Eventually, you may find yourself at the destination, but think about all you will have learned along the way!

## Establishing Your Mindset

Here is an additional resource to further your learning of this new way of thinking and being:

✦ *Zen Mind, Beginner's Mind: Informal Talks on Zen Meditation and Practice* by Shunryu Suzuki (Boston, MA: Shambala, 2011): This book features a series of short talks designed to teach mindfulness through zen principles.

# Open Journaling Space

# Open Journaling Space

# Open Journaling Space

_____

_____

_____

_____

_____

_____

_____

_____

_____

_____

_____

_____

_____

_____

# Open Journaling Space

# Open Journaling Space

_____

_____

_____

_____

_____

_____

_____

_____

_____

_____

_____

_____

_____

_____

# Part 3
# Meditate

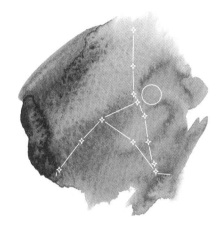

"When we change our thinking, we can actually change the solution."

—Raj Dhingra, 2012 TEDx Talk

When you practice mindfulness meditation, you relax, breathe, and focus on your thoughts and feelings in the moment. It's a way to be fully present, keeping your focus on every action you take, and it's a deeply rewarding practice. But it's also a solitary self-reflection exercise.

Edtech yoga combines breath, stretching, and meditation to create a holistic practice that helps educators to grow and achieve their goals. The breath helps with self-reflection, stretching helps create an action plan, and meditation helps to center you.

In our edtech yoga practice, when we talk about meditation, we want you to develop a healthy mindset that encourages growth. We start with self-reflection and then go further by giving thoughtful feedback to aid in reflection. From there, we encourage you to share the knowledge you've gained through this process with others in the edtech community. Your insights are too valuable to keep to yourself!

In chapter seven, we talk about how self-reflection is critical to the meditative process. Self-reflection is an individual activity, but you can also ask others to contribute to your self-reflection. In chapter eight, we discuss the different forms that meaningful feedback can take, including receiving and providing feedback to others. And in chapter nine, we encourage you to share your knowledge and insights with others, reinforcing the importance of contributing to the edtech community to keep the cycle of knowledge fresh and thriving.

# ISTE Standards for Educators That Connect to Part 3

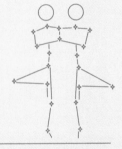

## 4. COLLABORATOR

**Educators dedicate time to collaborate with both colleagues and students to improve, practice, discover, and share resources and ideas, and solve problems. Educators:**

**4a**

Dedicate planning time to collaborate with colleagues to create authentic learning experiences that leverage technology.

**4b**

Collaborate and colearn with students to discover and use new digital resources and [to] diagnose and troubleshoot technology issues.

**4c**

Use collaborative tools to expand students' authentic, real-world learning experiences by engaging virtually with experts, teams, and students, locally and globally.

**4d**

Demonstrate cultural competency when communicating with students, parents, and colleagues and interact with them as cocollaborators in student learning.

## 7. ANALYST

**Educators understand and use data to drive their instruction and support students in achieving their learning goals. Educators:**

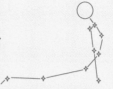

| 7a | 7b | 7c |
|---|---|---|
| Provide alternative ways for students to demonstrate competency and reflect on their learning using technology. | Use technology to design and implement a variety of formative and summative assessments that accommodate learner needs, provide timely feedback to students, and inform instruction. | Use assessment data to guide progress and communicate with students, parents, and education stakeholders to build student self-direction. |

# Self-Reflection

"When teachers stop learning, so do students."

—Jim Knight, *Unmistakable Impact: A Partnership Approach
for Dramatically Improving Instruction*

elf-reflection gives us insight into our thoughts and aspirations. The more thorough the process of self-reflection, the better we recognize our thoughts, feelings, values, and beliefs for what they really are. Self-reflection even prompts some individuals to question and restructure their entire belief system! What's more, the meditative process encourages you to re-evaluate your principles and core values in a nonjudgmental manner. Meditative reflection also helps us recall our short- and long-term goals.

We must welcome self-reflection as an opportunity for change—a chance to develop ourselves and our practice and to learn new things. This chapter begins by talking about being ready for change and about self-reflection. But the most productive self-reflection includes compassion and gratitude, so remember to be kind to yourself as you reflect.

## Are You Ready to Change?

How do you know if you are ready for change? Answering this question alone begins with self-reflection. Being able to look inside and reflect on oneself allows for a better sense of what needs to change. You must first know where you are coming from before you decide where you need to go.

In his book *Theory U: Leading from the Future as It Emerges,* Otto Scharmer (2009) theorizes that we are not one but *two* selves. One of our selves is the result of our past experiences and the other is our future possibility. He shares a theory of self-actualization and transformation whereby individuals go through a process of letting go of everything that isn't essential and developing an "open mind" through embracing curiosity, an "open heart" through feeling compassion, and an "open will" through showing courage (Scharmer, 2018, p. 30). Likewise, as we come closer to our destination in this learning journey, it's important to be present with both of our selves. According to Scharmer (2009, p. 42–43), we can reinvent ourselves and innovate by letting go of our past *self* (with a lowercase "s") and welcoming our future *Self* (with a capital S), inviting growth at the deepest level until that Self becomes our reality.

Humans are creatures of habit, so we tend to see everything through the lens of our past experiences. This mindset is a bit narrow, stemming from conditions and strategies that already occurred and not allowing much scope for innovation. When we repeat what we know or force a single solution because it worked in the past (without reconsidering the current landscape and scope of creative options), we are stuck in the *self.* Alternately, when we self-reflect and continuously reinvent ourselves for the purpose of improving our practice, we break free from the known and broaden our perspectives, thinking positively about the future (even when we initially think that our ideas are impossible to implement). As we open up and welcome our *Self,* we see things differently; we act as design thinkers and confront obstacles, creating new ways of seeing how we can do things differently to meet our objective.

# *Meditation Prompt*

## Being Open

As you consider Scharmer's Theory U, how could you best practice having an open mind, open heart, and open will when teaching and learning?

Throughout our life, we keep changing our identity; it's not a fixed thing. Real change happens at the level of our personal identity. Change is a choice—it is intentional (Bodell, 2012). The important learning here is that it is entirely possible to modify ourselves to be more aligned with who we want to be (Costa & Garmston, 2016) and with our emerging self. Everyone has the potential to extend their capacity and become more flexible.

We are ready to change when we can look forward with ambition and hope and leave behind cynicism and judgment. We are ready to change when we listen in order to understand rather than listening to respond. We are ready to change when we seek cognitive conflict (new information that challenges our beliefs), embrace divergent thinking (seeking as many solutions as possible), and push the limits of our thinking to open up horizons instead of building walls to protect our ideas.

## Forms of Self-Reflection

There are many different forms of self-reflection. You might adopt a formal self-reflection cycle (through your appraisal cycles, at the end of every teaching unit you complete, by using tools and strategies such as thinking routines every week, and so on); or you might be more casual in your process by striving to reflect when you feel a need or by doing self-reflecting so often that you develop an automatic mindset that becomes part of everything you do.

In yoga, you must be open to the challenge of each individual pose and also be willing to let go of your expectations of what you might accomplish or do. The same is true for self-reflection. We need to acknowledge our limitations and feelings, but also, in recognizing that vulnerability, cultivate the will to learn. Reflection is metacognitive; it's an inner process of thinking about our thinking! As we question and observe ourselves thinking, we make mental realizations about things we like or don't like about our teaching and learning and can then decide ways to modify ourselves to be a better version of ourselves. For example, at the end of a unit, when we self-reflect and realize that there were things that didn't go well, instead of ignoring these things and moving on, we can explore this vulnerability and understand the causes of the problem. We can unpack and analyze these factors, re-examining what is important to us and how we can adopt new strategies to improve in the future, when similar situations arise.

To develop the habit of self-reflection, we must remove our ego and think honestly about where we are and where we want to be. We must be flexible in our thinking by looking at the details as well as the big picture and by looking at ourselves from both of these perspectives. We must let go of our worries about external gratification—how we compare to others—and embrace openness. Don't be critical of yourself or your thoughts in the moment. Don't concern yourself with what others are doing or what they might be thinking. Acknowledge your limitations and feelings, and embrace your vulnerabilities. Self-reflection offers an opportunity to develop oneself and become increasingly autonomous as individuals.

The down side: self-reflection is not a one-time occurrence, and that can make it challenging. Just like yoga, it is a continual experience that must be practiced on a regular basis to be meaningful and effective. There is a reason we call it yoga "practice"—because you are always practicing. There is no "winning" or graduating in yoga, as there is always something more that you can do. But the more you self-reflect, the better you get in your practice.

Remember that you cannot do everything right away. You cannot go from nonstretching to bendy in one day. There are limitations and things will get in the way. But that is okay; it is all part of the journey, all part of the learning process. Rest assured that as you exercise, you will become increasingly flexible.

The following Take a Breath exercise provides tips for ways to practice self-reflection, and the edtech props suggest easy ways to self-reflect regularly.

## Take a Breath

### Quick Tips for How to Self-Reflect

Here are four ideas for easy self-reflection:

**1. Keep a journal.** Choose the format that works best for you (hand-written, typed, recorded, etc.) and journal on a regular basis. Reflective questions for journaling might include:

✦ How did my lesson go today? What went well and what might I consider improving upon?

✦ How did students react to the lesson?

✦ Did students seem engaged and motivated to learn during the lesson?

✦ Were the learning objectives met? What learning occurred?

✦ What evidence of learning did I observe or record? How might I use that data to prepare my next lesson?

At the end of a teaching unit, week, or quarter, go back and reread your journal entries. Spend some time reflecting on your past self, then write a self-reflection journal entry about this process.

**2. Conduct peer observation.** You can learn a lot by watching other educators. Even though time is a limited commodity in schools, try to get out of your classroom occasionally to conduct peer observations. And when you are observing your peers, think about what lessons you might take from their teaching. Don't try to copy your peers; rather, find ways to adapt their strengths or positive attributes to your teaching style and classroom.

**3. Record your lessons.** Make a video of yourself teaching, then watch the video and take notes. Reflect on how the lesson went. (You may have a specific aspect you'd like to target, or you could simply let ideas emerge as you watch.)

**4. Schedule time for self-reflection.** In your lesson plans or schedule for the workweek, include time for self-reflection and commit to maintaining this practice.

## *Edtech Props*

### Creative Writing

Creative writing is a wonderful reflective practice that we all can benefit from. And there is no need to put yourself into a "talented writer" box to do so; writing can be as simple as keeping a gratitude journal, adding one sentence about something you are grateful for each day. This is a great way to reflect on your day from a positive angle. You might be surprised that something that seemed to go wrong in your day actually transformed into an opportunity for growth. This practice also helps us to make decisions and take actions that foster our development. For instance, when journaling becomes a conscious habit, we automatically remind ourselves about who we are and who we are aspiring to become, reflecting on those actions that will bring us closer to our goal.

If you are not so keen on journaling, perhaps you can take five minutes every day to write down what you achieved that day—something we often overlook. We maintain a to-do list, crossing out things as we go but adding just as many—the list never goes away (the nature of life)! Always thinking of what *needs to be* done, we spend very little time acknowledging all the things that *have been* done, and that should change. You deserve to celebrate your achievements!

## Reflecting with Colleagues and Others

It is important to develop connections with other educators at multiple levels. Developing meaningful relationships with colleagues not only helps you stay connected but can help you grow as an educator. If you have a personal connection with a colleague, then it may be easier to work together on areas of growth. Find a supportive colleague or group of colleagues to collaborate with on your learning journey, as their insights can be a valuable part of your reflection. Also, there may be times when you are asked to help students or colleagues with their reflections, either informally or in a coaching situation, and we encourage you to do this. Collaboration builds something even greater than we can accomplish on our own.

As educators, we spend a lot of time giving and receiving information every day. However, our connections with others are more impactful when we listen and inquire. Coaching can be defined as this quest or journey of listening and inquiring to guide the coachee toward revealing his or her internal capital.

Educator Erin Lawson (district technology coach at Orchard Farm School District in Saint Charles, Missouri) shares her experience on developing the *sine qua non* condition for coaching to be successful:

> As a district technology coach, "technology" and "coach" seem to separate often. My role as a coach requires building and keeping trusting relationships with the educators in my district. Once a relationship is built, and I know the strengths and stretches of a person, the process of gently pushing that person to be the best educator begins. Technology integration happens naturally within that growth process.

When coaching, we thrive to support the coachee to think deeply and make new connections. For coaching to be effective, the coach has to suspend his or her judgments and actively engage in colearning and codeveloping. It all starts by listening, but this is a complex skill that is often taken for granted. Scharmer (2018) talks about "generative listening" as the highest level of listening. When we use this type of listening, we are intentional; we aren't passive or simply reconfirming what we already know. Instead, we listen with the intention to innovate. Generative listening is a very active listening style that allows space for the unknown and the new to emerge. It is a practice in mutual understanding and respect. Here are some tips for being an effective generative listener:

+ Let go of "just being a teacher" and embrace your singularities. When you listen to someone, do not listen from a formal distance but insert a bit of your personal self into it. Do you listen to your colleagues or students the way you listen to your parents or your own children? Give all your attention to the other person.

+ To truly open up to the other person, adopt an open nonverbal-communication style. Avoid crossing your arms and legs, and sit forward in your chair. Physically demonstrate that you are "receiving" what the person is saying rather than waiting for your turn to add something. Adopt a positive expression, nod, and capture the gestures of the other person to connect and develop the rapport that is necessary to have a harmonious conversation.

+ Remember that it's not about *you*. Remove the "noises" of your ego in your head (judgments and autobiographical dialogue) to listen as openly as possible.

+ See yourself as an instrument that pulls the message of the other person into reality. You can do this by echoing words or big concepts, or by paraphrasing.

When we converse with others, it's important that they feel listened to and understood. In order for them to feel listened to, we can paraphrase them. Costa and Garmston (2016) explain three different types of paraphrasing to achieve three different outcomes: (1) to acknowledge feelings and emotions, (2) to organize ideas and content, and (3) to highlight the main content to the abstraction level. Think about how it makes you feel when someone mirrors back your thinking, making your ideas and feelings visible. Paraphrasing is an incredible listening strategy that teaches us a lot about about another person in a present and respectful manner.

Coaching questions can also be very handy for exploring and identifying someone else's thinking. According to Garmston and Valerie von Frank (2012), in order to craft effective coaching questions that generate reflection and creativity (i.e., mediative questions), you need to ensure that those questions are:

+ Open-ended: Contrary to closed-ended questions, where answers are limited to yes or no, or are limited to short and surface-level responses, open-ended questions offer perspective to the coachee, allowing him or her to pause and think deeply before answering. These types of questions create the environment for the coachee to use his or her knowledge and feelings rather than directing him or her in a specific direction.

+ Invitational: The coach uses an approachable voice (a positive tone; a vocal inflection that goes up at the end of the question, in expectation of a response; and so on) and wording that captures a positive presupposition through the question (e.g., "As a committed professional, do you ... ?").

+ Exploratory: The coach uses tentative, unassuming language and plural forms to allow for a variety of responses, homing in on more specifics later if required (e.g., "What might be some of the ways you ... ?"). This allows him or her to keep the questions open-ended, not make any assumptions or judgments, and remain in the mode of listening for understanding. This opens up scope for a variety of answers and focuses the conversation on the big picture: the beliefs and vision of the coachee.

These three methods of inquiry have proven to deepen thinking and invite contribution from the point of view of the coachee, but there are many types of cognitive processes that can be enlisted when coaching. For example, Robert J. Marzano and John S. Kendall (2007) list the following:

+ knowledge retrieval (recall and execution),
+ comprehension (synthesis and representation),
+ analysis (matching, classifying, error analysis, generalizing, and specifying), and
+ knowledge utilization (decision-making, problem-solving, experimental inquiry, and investigation).

Instead of trying to be solution based, authentic coaching questions are intentional in the implied cognitive process. For example, if the intended function is to recall information, the question is created in such a way that the function is called up clearly (e.g., "What did you see your students do or say that made you ... ?").

Indeed, the coach does not try to fix a problem, push a hidden agenda, or evaluate the person; rather, the coach strives to genuinely support the coachee in thinking deeply and constructing new learning by himself/herself without interfering by providing answers, for example.

Use the following stretching exercise to create your own coaching questions.

# Stretching Exercise

## Crafting Coaching Questions

Given what you've just learned about the aspects of effective coaching questions (open-ended, invitational, and exploratory), how might you ask questions differently in the next few days? Contrast the questions you originally asked your students or colleagues against the same questions transformed into coaching questions.

First, take a look at the following two examples. Yes, the difference between them can sound wordy; however, the effect is significant. Try saying both versions out loud to hear the difference.

| Original Question | Coaching Question |
|---|---|
| (To a student) Can you speak louder, please? | As a learner who values communication, what are some of the ways you could invite everyone to be present with your contribution? |
| (To a colleague) Why did you change the instructions for the task at the last minute? | As an agile educator, what was some of the data you took into account when you decided to modify the task instructions? |

Now it's your turn to practice transforming your questions:

| Original Question | Coaching Question |
|---|---|
| (To a student) | |
| | |
| (To a colleague) | |
| | |

## *Inspiration*

### Learning to Reflect

Here are some additional resources to further your learning of this new way of thinking and being:

✦ *Becoming a Critically Reflective Teacher* by Stephen Brookfield (San Francisco: Jossey-Bass, 2017): This book provides you with many ways to consider your growth and take action to enhance your skills as a teacher.

✦ Activities from the Presencing Institute based on the implementation of Otto Sharmer's Theory U (presencing.org/#/resource/tools): These resources will allow you to practice various learning and leadership skills (i.e., listening, prototyping, and 4D mapping) while supporting you in your innovation journey.

# Meaningful Feedback

"Without feedback, there can be no transformative change."

— Brené Brown, *Daring Greatly*

M eaningful feedback is different from simple judgment or praise—it should not punish or reward. Rather, meaningful feedback should help the recipient grow as an individual through constructive comments or questions. This chapter delves into meaningful feedback by first addressing prior experiences with feedback that might influence your current feelings toward the term. Then it covers a variety of feedback forms that you might encounter as an educator in your efforts to deliver feedback to your students or colleagues. You might also want to consider how you can solicit and incorporate these meaningful feedback forms into your own practice in a productive way.

## Prior Experience with Feedback

Feedback is "information about others and ourselves, and about our thinking and behaviors" (Drago-Severson & Blum-DeStefano 2016, p. 17). Let's think back about your experience giving or receiving feedback in the past. What did it feel like to you when you received feedback? How did you feel after sharing feedback with someone else? You might have an anecdote popping up in your head; it could be a good or a bad memory. Explore this memory with the following meditation prompt, then try the "Exercise Your

Empathy" stretching exercise, which invites you to empathize with how your students might feel when they are receiving feedback.

# *Meditation Prompt*

## Recalling Your Experience with Feedback

Reflect on a memory of a prior experience with receiving feedback. Think about the specifics of the feedback—how it was given, how it made you feel, and how you reacted to the situation.

Now reflect on a memory of a prior experience with giving feedback. Think about the specifics of the feedback—what you said, how you said it, your intention in giving the feedback, and how it might have made the recipient feel.

# Stretching Exercise

## Exercising Your Empathy

As you think about your students' experience with feedback, try to remember back when you were a student receiving feedback. Try to recall your feelings about two particular instances of feedback given to you as a student—a positive instance and a negative one.

| A Negative Experience of Feedback | A Positive Experience of Feedback |
| --- | --- |
| | |

You may have noticed that most people, when receiving as well as providing feedback, feel vulnerable, and this vulnerability can be seen as a weakness or a strength. Looking at the half-full glass, we recognize that accepting this vulnerability only makes us more human and more flexible. One of the most useful tips to remember: assume positive intent, even if the feedback is not delivered in the best way. It's not always easy to do, especially when it comes from parents or supervisors. Alternately, feedback, when taken negatively, creates a defensive mechanism for the person receiving it, and there will likely be little growth.

We are often reluctant to create a culture of feedback in schools. According to Brown (2012), there is a negative assumption associated with feedback, as it is perceived to be a place of discomfort. Also, people may be unskilled in giving feedback or uncertain about how to provide feedback in ways that actually support growth. Paradoxically, though, feedback is something that everyone wants!

Earlier, we discussed the importance of risk-taking, the role of fear in boosting us to challenge ourselves, and the need for resilience and perseverance when stretching. Feedback has a place in this conversation, as developing a culture of timely, honest, and constructive feedback creates the ideal conditions for growth.

## Providing Feedback to Others

As we discuss in chapter seven, self-reflection is an important form of feedback to oneself; however, there are many ways that we can also provide reflections and feedback to others, helping them along in their stretching journey as well. If you are a classroom teacher, then you already provide feedback to your students every day. You may also be providing feedback to your colleagues.

Feedback can easily be misunderstood as suggestions or praise, or even criticism. While there are different, sometimes conflicting, definitions of feedback, we would like to talk about feedback as providing information to the person observed in order to support him/her in thinking and growing. For us, feedback is not evaluative. Furthermore, the way it is given matters a lot. For instance, nonverbal language contributes a great deal to how a person's words are perceived. A friendly face and tone both go a long way, particularly when dealing with sensitive statements about someone's performance. Because of the challenge that we tend to have when giving and receiving feedback, positive body language does wonders for increasing comfort level.

When it comes to providing feedback, we should be aware of the "culture of nice," which means simply praising others without providing meaningful data. Indeed, we could argue this is categorized as "feedback" but more as evaluation. One example of this is using the "sandwich" method of feedback delivery: sharing "needs improvement" feedback between two compliments, or exaggerating and overcomplimenting someone around the constructive feedback. Being overly nice can make your message unclear, and the fact is that providing productive feedback usually requires having challenging conversations. With feedback, however, comfort is not the aim; growth is! Going further, one way to provide feedback is by mirroring what someone is saying through listening and inquiring—two strategies of effective coaches.

## Different Forms of Feedback

According to Douglas Stone and Sheila Heen (2014), feedback can be distinguished by three different purposes: appreciation, coaching, and evaluation (p. 45). While all three are valuable, we need to be deliberate about when and how to use them:

+ **Appreciation:** When we provide appreciative feedback, we express gratefulness for the value that someone brings to the endeavor. This motivates and encourages.

+ **Coaching:** When we coach someone, we help identify challenging areas and support this person in finding the resourcefulness to overcome the problem. This increases self-directedness.

✦ **Evaluation:** When we evaluate someone, we often refer to standards and judge performance against those standards. This tells the person being evaluated where she or he stands.

Another interesting framework to consider as educators comes from the work of Costa and Garmston (2016), who identified five forms of feedback that can be utilized for different purposes. The authors divide the five forms into two categories: feedback that is evaluative (or judgmental) and feedback that is coaching (nonjudgmental). In the edtech props below, we share the five categories of feedback and give examples of each type.

### Forms of Feedback

The five forms of feedback were developed by Costa and Garmston (2016). The authors divide those forms into two main categories: judgmental and nonjudgmental feedback. When we place ourselves in the role of an evaluator, we often provide judgmental feedback, but when we are taking a coaching approach (more dynamic and centered around growth), we provide feedback that will, in turn, allow the coachee to make their own judgment about their performance. Within each category, we find further information that describes types of feedback we might already use in class or with colleagues. Take a moment to pay close attention to each one and attempt to choose mindfully and intentionally to reach your purpose.

*(continued on next page)*

| Evaluative (Judgmental Feedback) | | |
| --- | --- | --- |
| **Evaluations and Judgments** | **Personal Opinions and Preferences** | **Inferences, Causality, and Interpretation** |
| *Good job!* <br><br> *Well done!* | *I liked this lesson very much!* <br><br> *I appreciated the tool you used to engage students!* | *The video you showed in the beginning of the lesson supported students' understanding of the task.* |

| Coaching (Nonjudgmental Feedback) | |
| --- | --- |
| **Nonjudgmental Data** | **Mediative Questions** |
| *You organized three different learning centers for your students to engage with the material today.* | *What did you consider in your planning and lesson delivery to guide your decision on groupings and differentiated instruction?* |

According to this framework, when we evaluate someone, we might provide judgments, opinions, and inferences; however, if we choose to provide coaching feedback, we can use data and mediative questions to engage the person in making their own judgments, opinions, and inferences.

As we would like to provoke awareness and growth, the coaching form of feedback would be our preference here. We would like to enable the coachee (who can be a student or a colleague) to think deeply and make his or her own self-evaluation. In order to promote this approach, we will take a closer look at the two forms of feedback that support self-directedness: data-driven feedback and mediative questions.

## Data-Driven Feedback

Why is data the center of attention for educators in the digital age? Following the ISTE Standards for Educators and its seventh standard—Analyst—we understand and use learning data to support our students in achieving their goals. The focus is on developing self-directedness through deliberate planning, collecting, and handling of learning data. These data sources are useful to know where our students stand in their pathways to personal learning.

You may have heard about the "data rich, information poor" syndrome, or DRIP syndrome, that surrounds us nowadays: though we may have a lot of data, we may also have little understanding of its implications. Schools are no exception to this situation, and Garmston and Wellman (2016) remind us that "data have no meaning on their own" (p. 31). We make meaning out of the data we collect when people interact with it.

What is data? When we think of data, we might first think about numbers and scores; however, data comes in various forms, such as anecdotal notes, multimedia evidence, and student reflections. Stone and Heen (2014) also explain that data can include "anything directly observed," such as someone's behavior, statements, or tone (p. 54).

When it comes to feedback, we first need to understand which data is worth collecting and interpreting. We need to anticipate a goal and how collecting data around that goal might support us in assessing whether our purpose was achieved or not. And data can be quantitative or qualitative. In the context of teacher observation, if we want to collect nonjudgmental data, we might want to make a video of ourselves or have a colleague observe and take notes based on desired data points. After the observation, the observer can share the data with you, then you can make meaning of it through your own judgments, opinions, and inferences.

## Take a Breath

### Data, Data, Data

Some data-driven feedback examples:

✦ You worked about _____ minutes with student *x* _____.

✦ You spent about _____ minutes talking with the student.

✦ You initiated the student's physical movement in the classroom _____ times.

✦ You paused between _____ and _____ seconds between your questions and the student's answers.

✦ You stayed at your desk for _____ minutes, moved around the classroom for _____ minutes, and sat with _____ students for about _____ minutes each (or _____ minutes total).

## Mediative Questions

Feedback from others can come in the form of questions. Indeed, inquiring is a powerful way to guide people toward thinking deeply and making meaning on their own, without pushing a single perspective or giving them solutions. Mediative feedback is described in detail by Costa and Garmston (2016), who explain that "posing questions has the highest potential for developing self-directedness" (p. 53); questions provide "self-feedback" that helps the person being coached to construct meaning and then set goals to self-modify.

Questions act as feedback, because they call for specific cognitive processes that engage the coachee to think deeply and, through the conversation, develop new learnings. Some of the cognitive processes might include the ones described in Bloom's taxonomy, but we would like to draw particular attention to the six types of thinking as explained by Marzano and Kendall (2007): remembering, understanding, applying, analyzing, evaluating, and creating.

# *Stretching Exercise*

## Probing for Understanding

Practice listening and inquiring with your students, colleagues, and/or family members in simple ways. Active listening means probing for understanding and setting aside unproductive patterns of listening such as "autobiographical listening," "inquisitive listening," "mindreading," "solution listening," and "filtering" (Costa & Garmston, 2016, p. 7273). Keep the focus on the other person rather than thinking about what you want to say in response. For example, ask "What makes you say that?" or prompt them by saying, "Tell me more…"

# Receiving Feedback

Teachers are often quite hard on themselves, suffering from "impostorship" (Brookfield, 2017), which is a tendency to feel that they are ineffective and incompetent (p. 227). Have you ever experienced this feeling while teaching? Feeling a bit insecure is the proof that teachers are humble and critical. Fortunately, it is possible to overcome feelings of impostorship.

Earlier, we talked about practicing self-compassion, risk-taking, and embracing change through discomfort. To utilize these tools, we need an accurate picture of where we currently are in our teaching practices; our students might be the best resources to provide this information. Feedback from students might make us feel exposed and vulnerable, but if we establish trust with them, their honesty can bring up very useful data. While student-teacher evaluations are a common classroom practice, they are not often useful, because results come after the fact (Brookfield, 2017). Even so, there are other ways to receive feedback. And timing can be everything! Receiving feedback on the fly supports teachers to adjust their teaching and improvise teaching techniques immediately, in real time. The edtech props below can be used to receive feedback from students in class in the moment.

# Edtech Props

## Receiving Feedback from Students

We provide feedback to students daily. Here are some tools that can support us in delivering feedback or promoting student reflection or peer-assessment, thereby allowing our learners to think about their learning and how they might improve.

| Ways to Receive Feedback from Students | Possible Tools |
|---|---|
| Back channel: Create a back channel that you keep live throughout your lesson and that students can use anytime they need to share their thoughts, doubts, successes.<br><br>(Socrative offers the ability to create short-answer anonymous quizzes.) | **Socrative**<br>Socrative.com<br><br>**Padlet**<br>padlet.com |
| Prior-knowledge assessment or exit ticket: Before starting the lesson or at the end of the lesson, ask students a question about the content to verify where they are in their learning. (Note: open-ended questions will provide more accurate results than multiple-choice questions, which can be answered randomly.)<br><br>(Google Classroom's assessments allow students to edit their answers but not see their classmates' answers.)<br><br>(Google Forms allows teachers to view student responses individually or collectively, view responses in a spreadsheet or visual format [e.g., bar graphs, pie charts], and create a peer-assessment workflow.) | **Google Classroom**<br>classroom.google.com<br><br>**Google Forms**<br>docs.google.com/forms |

| Ways to Receive Feedback from Students | Possible Tools |
|---|---|
| Three cards: After the lesson, present students with three basic assessments, either online or offline. You can use services like Padlet or provide each student with three cards or Post-it Notes to discuss the following: <br><br> Card 1: One thing I learned . . . <br><br> Card 2: One thing I am unsure about . . . <br><br> Card 3: One thing I want to learn . . . <br><br> Give students a few minutes to respond with a short statement for each discussion point and then let them share their responses with three different learning partners, having them move around the classroom to explain their point and listen to others. You can move around the classroom to listen to the different conversations. At the end of the class, collect the cards or go to the online resource and review their responses for further reflection. | **Padlet** <br> Padlet.com <br><br> (This can also be an offline activity.) |
| Grown answers: The use of word-cloud tools such as AnswerGarden can be a powerful way to find out the big idea, big concept, or general feeling of the students. <br><br> (Services like AnswerGarden take keywords that students contribute to create a word cloud, enlarging repeated answers to demonstrate the general consensus.) | **AnswerGarden** <br> AnswerGarden.ch |

*(continued on next page)*

| Ways to Receive Feedback from Students | Possible Tools |
|---|---|
| Thumbs-up or numbers: Ask students to respond in real time by making a physical gesture (thumbs-up or -down) or a virtual one (using Pear Deck or Plickers, for instance) to indicate where they are in their learning. | **Pear Deck**<br>PearDeck.com<br><br>**Plickers**<br>Get.Plickers.com |
| Corners or scale: Students can physically move about the classroom to "named" or labeled places that correspond with where they are in their understanding of the concept being taught. This can be done with labeled corners of the classroom or with either side of an imaginary scale on the floor, which has its two opposing sides labeled. | (This is an offline activity.)<br><br>This can be done digitally, too, by asking students to place a unique symbol that represents them in a GoogleDrawing in which all students have edit access, for example. |
| Private journals: Provide a space for students to share private feedback with you.<br><br>(This can be a one-on-one discussion thread in an LMS [learning management system] like Google Classroom, a class notebook in OneNote or another note-taking tool, or a composition notebook, which wouldn't require internet access.) | **Google Classroom**<br>classroom.google.com<br><br>**Canvas**<br>CanvasLMS.com<br><br>**PowerSchool**<br>PowerSchool.com<br><br>**OneNote**<br>products.office.com/en-us/onenote/digital-note-taking-app<br><br>(This can also be an offline activity.) |

Another interesting way to process feedback is through "postparation" (Young, 2011, p. 59). Instead of focusing on planning the next lesson by *pre*paring (which can make us focus our attention on the curriculum alone), we can *post*pare our lesson planning based on the feedback received in the previous class.

# Meditation Prompt

## Seeing Feedback in a New Light

After learning, relearning, or unlearning the elements of effective feedback, where are you in your thinking about the way you perceive feedback when it is given to you and when you offer it to someone (your students, a colleague, etc.)?

_____

_____

_____

_____

## *Inspiration*

### Listening for Learning *or* Giving and Receiving Feedback

Here are some additional resources to further your learning of this new way of thinking and being:

✦ *Tell Me So I Can Hear You: A Developmental Approach to Feedback for Educators* by Eleanor Drago-Severson and Jessica Blum-DeStefano (Cambridge, MA: Harvard Education Press, 2016): This book will help you develop ways to provide feedback. It focuses on leadership skills, how to deliver supportive feedback, and how to personalize the way it is delivered, meeting the recipient's needs and generating growth.

✦ *Thanks for the Feedback: The Science and Art of Receiving Feedback Well (Even When It Is Off Base, Unfair, Poorly Delivered, and Frankly, You're Not in the Mood)* by Douglas Stone and Sheila Heen (New York: Penguin Group, 2014): This book will help you see feedback differently and regain control by focusing on how you receive feedback.

# Sharing Our Journey with Others

"Preparation is obviously important, but at some point, you must stop preparing content and start preparing mindset. You have to shift from what you'll say to how you'll say it."

—Amy Cuddy, *Presence: Bringing Your Boldest Self to Your Biggest Challenges*

By now, you've learned that self-reflection is mostly an individual activity. However, as chapter eight discussed, giving and receiving meaningful feedback can inform self-reflection. Building on that idea further, in this chapter, you will learn about how to share your learning journey with others—an important milestone that allows us to learn from each other's experiences. Even when you think you might not be ready to contribute and would rather continue observing others' shares, this chapter will make you realize that sharing is not about showing off; sharing is a generous act, even if it is a bit daunting. When you share your learning journey, you extend your circle of influence, contributing at a larger scale. Educators often feel isolated within the classroom, as they do not always have like-minded colleagues to share their ideas with, but they do not need to be that way within the global teaching community. How do they reach out to connect? Sharing can occur in formal ways (such as presenting at conferences), informal ways (through social-media channels), and more. As in the classroom, creativity and stretching also apply to sharing and building community!

# Conferences: Learning from Others

Attending conferences can be a valuable learning opportunity, from participating in the more organized conference programming to casually networking with other conference attendees. And scale is another consideration. Conferences can be large, like ISTE's annual conference, or more intimate, like Edcamps and other "unconferences." Often, there are opportunities to attend conferences virtually if you are unable to travel.

Not sure where to start? Get inspired by attending one of the top edtech conferences in the following list! Once you choose a conference, think about stretching yourself by presenting, which we will talk about more in the next section.

## Top Edtech Conferences

| Conference | Timeline | Location |
|---|---|---|
| **ISTE (International Society for Technology in Education) conference** conference.ISTE.org | Yearly— late June | Various cities in the United States |
| **SXSW EDU conference and festival** SXSWedu.com | Yearly— early March | Austin, Texas (US) |
| **CoSN (Consortium for School Networking) annual conference** CoSNconference.org | Yearly— early April | Various cities in the United States |

| Conference | Timeline | Location |
| --- | --- | --- |
| **Spring CUE (Computer-Using Educators) conference** CUE.org/spring | Yearly—mid-March | Various cities in California and Nevada (US) |
| **FETC (Future of Education Technology Conference)** FETC.org | Yearly—late January | Florida (US) |
| **EdTechTeam events (bootcamps, keynotes, summits, workshops)** EdTechTeam.com/events | Varies by location | Global |
| **Edcamp** Edcamp.org | Varies by location | Various cities in the United States |
| **Global Education Conference** GlobalEducationConference.org | Varies—virtual (online) platform | Global (online) |
| **21st Century Learning conference** 21CLHK.org | Yearly—varies | Hong Kong (China) |

# Conferences: Presenting and Building a Network

We would like to shout it out: *Don't wait for your work to feel "perfect" to share it!* Learning happens in the doing; and if you are passionate about something you learned, you will have great stories that others will want to hear. Go out there and tell the world about your experiences! Every time you hold yourself back because of fear, you become less flexible and more prone to being passive. However, when you have the courage to be vulnerable and put yourself out there, you might be surprised by how many participants thank you for your authenticity, generosity, and insight.

There are many conferences to which you can apply to be a presenter; so once you find one that suits you, don't hesitate. This is yet another opportunity to stretch! In the process of planning your session, you will refine your craft and build new learning; in the delivery stage, you will experience excitement and pride; and in the reflection part, you will become aware of things that you might like to improve upon. When you present at conferences, you become part of a group of proactive educators who take risks and aspire to make a difference in the educational world. Eventually, as you spend time with other presenters with more or less experience, you will build and find your tribe! It can be rewarding to share with less-experienced educators but also to enter a world where you are considered a leader and you feel that you are making an impact. Just go for it!

Keep in mind, too, that a presentation does not require standing on a large stage in front of a faceless crowd. There are many different types of presentations that allow you to share your knowledge, as the following list demonstrates.

+ Short talks (e.g., Ignite, PechaKucha, TED Talks): Afraid of public speaking? Try doing it for a shorter amount of time first! Right now, short talks are a popular format for presenting. Fast, structured talks give many individuals the chance to share powerful ideas in a short amount of time. For example, PechaKucha 20x20 allows presenters to show twenty slides, with twenty seconds to talk about each slide.

+ Poster sessions: Poster sessions can be a great introduction to presenting if you are afraid of speaking in front of a large audience. A poster session still requires you to talk to other people but in a more informal, often one-on-one or small group setting. You will still want to prepare talking points, but your audience walks by and connects with you if they are interested in your topic or are drawn in by your visuals. Then you start a conversation with them. Be prepared for questions and have strong visuals and resources to support your talking points, drawing people to learn more about your poster presentation.

✦ Workshops: Do you have a great lesson or tool that you want to share but aren't sure how to convey that in a traditional presentation? Consider leading a workshop in which you share your skills or teach others how to implement the same great lesson. Workshops vary in length, but all are hands-on, with presenters leading participants through an activity.

✦ Webinars or virtual conferences: Don't have a big professional-development or travel budget? There are many virtual conferences that provide presenting opportunities in a more affordable format.

# Stretching Exercise

## Presentation Brainstorming

You may be thinking, "What could I possibly do a presentation on that others would enjoy?" Well, here is a space for you to brainstorm some ideas!

Use a stopwatch or set a timer for sixty seconds. In those sixty seconds, write down as many ideas for presentations as you can. Don't worry if they are "good" or "bad" ideas; just write down everything! You can sort it all out later, with further reflection.

_____

_____

_____

---

---

---

---

---

## Using Social Media to Connect

There are other ways to share your learning journey than presenting. One easy way is to share online through social media—an outlet with many benefits. You can connect with other like-minded educators, find people with whom you can collaborate on projects, have conversations around a certain topic, and share project ideas and resources. A major social-media tool that is used by educators in the edtech world is Twitter. Even if you're not already a user of Twitter, you likely know that this app and website allows users to share messages that have up to 280 characters, with the option of adding links, pictures, and videos. Depending on how many people you choose to follow on Twitter, it can end up being a constant stream of information. You can also make and organize lists of Twitter feeds around certain topics/hashtags. (On Twitter, users add hashtags to their tweets to identify that they are about a specific topic.) For example, you could make a list of ISTE presenters, a list of local educators, or a list of AR/VR experts.

**Caitlin McLemore**
@EdTechCaitlin

"Multicultural education includes but is much more than content integration" (Banks, 2006). YES. Looking forward to an interesting summer course. #BookSnaps #JHUEdD18 #gradschool

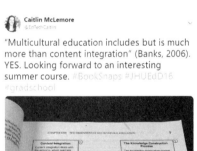

12:43 PM – 3 Jun 2018

When conversations or tweet chats center on a specific hashtag, they can be slow chats that happen asynchronously or chats scheduled to happen at a specific date and time. The example tweet shown here is from an asynchronous chat intended for graduate students attending a certain graduate program (hashtag "JHUEdD16"). The tweet also uses the hashtag "BookSnaps" to share about a book that the user is reading for class. Cybrary Man (cybraryman.com/chats.html) has a great list of education- and edtech-focused Twitter chats and hashtags.

Now that we have covered the basics of Twitter, what are other social-media tools that you might use as an educator? Like Twitter, Instagram is an app that allows users to share photos and videos. Instagram also uses hashtags to identify topics within each post, and you can follow topics or users that you are interested in. Snapchat is an app that allows users to share photos and videos, but the posts only last for a few seconds and only stay on the app for a maximum of twenty-four hours. Snapchat first became popular among teens, but now it is used by educators to share what is going on in their classrooms, their thoughts on education, and their experiences with trying new resources and tools. Finally, there is the Facebook app and website. Often, edtech companies or organizations have Facebook pages that you can follow for new information and news. Also, you can use Facebook to connect with other educators on a more personal level.

One great example of educators using Snapchat for learning is #BookSnaps. Started by Tara Martin, #BookSnaps is available for students and teachers to have casual conversations about the books they are reading. In an Ignite session at ISTE 2017, Tara Martin shared that she wanted her students to be excited about reading, and using Snapchat worked! #BookSnaps has now expanded from Snapchat to Instagram and Twitter.

The great thing about these different social-media tools is that there is so much out there—you get to pick and choose what you are interested in following. Just be careful not to overwhelm yourself. The information stream is constant and ever changing, so do not try to consume it all. Rather, use the organizational tools on each site like followers, hashtags, and lists to stay on top of things.

An additional word of caution: social media can be a great and powerful tool for connecting and learning, but be sure to use it wisely. If you have a personal account on one of these sites, consider creating a separate professional account. Be mindful of what you post on your public accounts. Think about what would you want your students to see versus what you would want your friends to see. Additionally, check with your place of employment about any social-media policies that they have in place. Also, be very careful when sharing about students. Be sure that if you post a picture of a student or your student's work, you have parental and school permission first. Sharing is great, but respecting others' privacy needs to be the priority.

## Social Media for Educators

| Social-Media Tool | What It Does |
|---|---|
| **Twitter**<br>Twitter.com | Share messages up to 280 characters with optional hashtags, links, photos, and videos; direct (private) messaging is also an option |
| **Instagram**<br>Instagram.com | Share photos and videos; direct (private) messaging is also an option |
| **Snapchat**<br>Snapchat.com | Share photos and quick videos that are available for viewing for up to twenty-four hours; direct (private) messaging is also an option |
| **Facebook**<br>Facebook.com | Share longer posts with optional hashtags, links, photos, and videos; direct (private) messaging is also an option |

# *Meditation Prompt*

## The Ripple Effect of Social Media

What social-media tools might appeal to you in your practice of stretching yourself? How might these be used to share your ideas with others and make a positive impact?

_____

_____

_____

_____

_____

_____

_____

_____

_____

_____

# Publishing and Sharing Online

While connecting and sharing on social media is convenient, sometimes you will want to share more than 280 characters or a few photos at a time. Maybe you designed a really great lesson plan that you want to explain further, or maybe you tried out a new tech gadget that you want to review; or maybe you have lots of opinions on the edtech and educational landscape that you think would be valuable to pass along. Fortunately, there are more robust online tools for sharing with others than the social-media tools highlighted in the last section.

One of the best practices when curating edtech tools is to make your own collection of resources online. And once you start curating, you can review and share your feedback with others; then you are not simply consuming but creating, participating, and supporting others in the edtech community as well. One simple way to do this is to share a list of resources that you created on social media by blogging or posting the list on your website. If you don't want to make an entire list but have one great resource that you would like to share with others, you can contribute your reviews of individual tools on their sites and then share a link to that review on any relevant social-media outlets.

Some ideas for sharing online in a longer format include blogging, sketch-noting, vlogging, or creating a YouTube channel. Publishing content in one of these formats allows you to develop your voice as an educator, giving others the opportunity to learn from you. Publishing/sharing content on a regular (or irregular!) basis means that you are connecting with and contributing to the global community. Publishing content online also provides an opportunity for self-reflection that others can benefit from too.

## Publishing Online

| Edtech Tool | What It Does |
|---|---|
| **Common Sense Education** commonsense.org/education/reviews/all **ISTE Edtech Advisor** iste.org/membership/edtechadvisor | Educator reviews of resources (apps, websites, etc.) |
| **Diigo** Diigo.com **Feedly** Feedly.com **eduClipper** eduClipper.net **Pinterest** Pinterest.com **Scoop.it!** Scoop.it **Symbaloo** blog.symbaloo.com/what-is-symbaloo | Bookmarking/resource-curation tools |
| **Periscope** pscp.tv | Live video sharing |

*(continued on next page)*

| Edtech Tool | What It Does |
|---|---|
| Tumblr<br>Tumblr.com<br><br>Blogger<br>Blogger.com | Blogging platforms |
| YouTube<br>YouTube.com | Platform for creating an online video channel |

Remember to do what works for you. Be authentic to yourself and your style. A wonderful benefit to the digital age is the plethora of options available to you. Try them all, but don't force yourself to use a tool you don't like just because it is trendy.

## Meditation Prompt

### Publishing with Purpose

What edtech publishing tools are you interested in using? What kinds of resources would you like to share, and what could be your focus/topic?

_____

_____

_____

_____

_____

_____

_____

_____

_____

_____

_____

## *Inspiration*

### Getting Your Voice Out There

Here are some additional resources to further your learning of this new way of thinking and being:

✦ *TED Talks: The Official TED Guide to Public Speaking* by Chris Anderson: This resource offers practical tips for public speaking, including preparation, delivery, and analysis. Though the author focuses on TED Talks, the guide is useful for all public-speaking situations.

✦ *Weekend Language: Presenting with More Stories and Less PowerPoint* by Andy Craig and Dave Yewman: This slim and sharp book will help you rethink your PowerPoints and traditional ways of sharing ideas, and consider how to spread your message wider with simple communication tricks and tips.

# *Conclusion*

"We recognize understanding through a flexible performance....
Understanding shows its face when people can think and act flexibly around
what they know. In contrast, when a learner cannot go beyond rote and
routine thought and action, this signals lack of understanding. *To understand
means to be able to perform flexibly.*"

—David Perkins (1998, p. 42; author emphasis)

## Appreciate Growth and Learning

Congratulations on making it this far in your stretching journey! Hopefully, through reading and interacting with this book, you were able to stretch further as an educator. The personality quiz you took in the introduction gave you a framework for reading as you learned to breathe, stretch, and meditate with us. Take a moment to look back at the results of the quiz you took in the beginning of the book and think about how you feel about those results now. How might you reflect on your stretching journey? We hope you feel more confident about your flexibility power and will persist to keep fit!

Take a moment to appreciate your growth and learning. This conclusion will provide some final words of advice and final reflective activities. Though you have read through this book once, you should not put it away and forget about it. If you completed all of the journaling and stretching activities, you have concrete ideas for how to take action. Reference these frequently as you try new things in your classroom. Reread chapters when needed. We want to continue to be a part of your journey as an edtech educator! Continue the conversation with us in the "Stretch Yourself" section of our website, NoBordersLearning.com: noborderslearning.com/stretch-yourself.

## Cyclical Growth

Think back to where you were before you started reading this book and ask yourself these questions: "What if I were starting to read this book now; how would this experience compare? Where am I in my thinking compared to when I started reading this book? What has changed? What about myself and my journey has been clarified or deepened?"

This is your time to acknowledge and honor your learning by going back to the introduction and taking the personality quiz again. Push yourself gently, to show your progress, as you might surprise yourself. Teachers are often very harsh on themselves; they are shy or afraid to share their success, thinking this will be misinterpreted as arrogance. Austin Kleon (2014) sums it up when he declares that "the worst troll is the one that lives in your head" (p. 155). It's time to let yourself be *you* and to celebrate your agility. After completing the personality quiz a second time, regardless of where you stand now, take credit for your growth.

Remember the importance of self-reflection in your stretching journey. Establishing a consistent practice of self-reflection will help you to continue to grow and stretch. Your journey is never over; there is always room for growth—room for new strategies and new tools to learn! If you need help to refocus on your stretching journey, consider revisiting chapter seven for specific self-reflection strategies.

## What Does It Mean to Be Flexible?

Here are some criteria to keep in mind as you continue to stretch yourself:

+ Allow yourself to take risks—innovation blooms in discomfort.

+ Handle problems and bounce back. In times when things don't go as planned, find the strength to develop resilience, perseverance, and stamina; then pick yourself up so that you're ready for the next new adventure.

✦ Welcome other viewpoints. For example, listen actively, inquire and receive feedback positively, and practice compassion.

✦ Observe yourself from another perspective. Monitor yourself, think about what you would advise to improve and stretch yourself, and then take the appropriate action(s).

✦ Zoom in and out of a situation to look at it from different angles. Understanding the big picture as well as the finite details develops agility when taking action(s).

✦ Be positive, but remain vulnerable. It's crucial that being positive does not equate to hiding your feelings. When you have an emotional response to a situation, try to identify the feeling you're experiencing and acknowledge it by practicing self-compassion. Slowly, you will find the resourcefulness to overcome the negative association and embrace your authentic self, stretching you to shine even brighter.

✦ Let go of the old to welcome the new. Letting go is important, as it makes space for new ideas. This doesn't mean that you have to get rid of everything in your current toolbox; it just means that you can extend your repertoire of strategies and, in the process, discard what no longer serves your teaching practice.

✦ Grasp lifelong learning by embodying an eagerness to learn. This mindset will inspire others in turn.

✦ Embrace change and be contemporary. The digital age requires us to constantly adapt new tools, open up our horizons, and welcome innovation.

✦ Accept responsibility by exercising your rights and staying true to your values. Be principled and self-reflective as you continue to stretch your teaching practice.

+ Think critically. Resist the urge to copy others by finding your unique voice within the context and complexity of your situation. Adapt the experiences and input of others to match the needs of your classroom, and not the other way around.

+ Communicate genuinely, with honesty, sincerity, and transparency.

+ Practice self-directedness and conscious action. Being deliberate and intentional in planning, doing, and reflecting is the key to this process.

## Farewell

If we were to summarize the three parts of the book with mottos, we could say:

+ Part 1: Breathe—It's not about imitating; it's about finding your unique "you."
+ Part 2: Stretch—It's not about reaching mastery; it's about experiencing the ongoing process that leads to mastery.
+ Part 3: Meditate—It's not about you or me; it's about building genuine relationships that stretch and enhance you *and* me.

In writing this book, we kept thinking about you! We tried to create a personalized learning environment that is interactive and nonlinear, where you can choose to hack the book and make it yours, just like you would with technology.

As deliberate contributors, we constantly reflect and try to walk the walk. We hope we've modeled best practices and led by example. Throughout the writing of this book, we tinkered and learned, relearned, and unlearned things we assumed we knew about teaching and learning! *Stretch Yourself* is not meant to "tell" you how to be; rather, it's the product of our deep, reflective practice. Writing it has been as much a stretching process for us as we hope it has been for you in reading it. May you use it as a tool to enhance your practice, not dictate it. *You* are still the best captain of your learning journey!

We hope you felt our humanity and sincerity in these pages, as we really care about you and want the very best for you. We gave you what we could at this stage of our own stretching journey, and we invite you to continue your journey with us through the "Stretch Yourself" section on our website, NoBordersLearning .com: nobordentslearning.com/stretch-yourself.

There is no badge, no certificate, no external recognition for completing this book, yet we hope that you find in yourself a deep sense of satisfaction and pride because you did. Like Kleon says, "validation is for parking" (2012, p. 111); we don't need someone else to tell us where we are in our growth and learning in order to embrace and own it! If you felt a boost in your self-confidence through this book, don't worry; feeling empowered isn't going to transform you into an arrogant person. You have the right to feel the magic force of "I can do this!" and the desire to tell the world—so go for it! You will likewise inspire and empower others when you show your work.

Once again, congratulations on your learning! We wish you all the very best in continuing your stretching practice, and we gift you with this parting mantra and a final meditation prompt. Use the latter to think about how your level of flexibility changed throughout this learning journey.

Until we meet again . . .

"You are the most talented, most interesting, and most extraordinary person in the universe. And you are capable of amazing things."

—Emmet, *The LEGO Movie* (2014)

# Meditation Prompt

## Reflecting by Going Back to the Start

An appropriate reflective and metacognitive thinking routine is the "I Used to Think..., Now I Think..." exercise (Ritchhart et al., 2011). Use it to recall what you were thinking about your flexibility before reading this book and what you are thinking now.

| I used to think . . . | Now I think . . . |
|---|---|
|  |  |

# Inspiration

## Being Bold!

Here are some additional resources to further your learning of this new way of thinking and being:

✦ *The Places that Scare You* by Pema Chodron (Boston, MA: Shambala Publications, 2001): Chodron provides tools for dealing with the difficult or "scary" moments in our lives in order to discover growth and improvement.

✦ *Daring Greatly: How the Courage to Be Vulnerable Transforms the Way We Live, Love, Parent, and Lead* by Brené Brown (New York: Random House, 2012): Brown imparts research-based knowledge in a relatable way. *Daring Greatly* focuses on vulnerability and developing the courage to be vulnerable in order to enact true change in ourselves and in others.

# Open Journaling Space

---

---

---

---

---

---

---

---

---

---

---

---

---

---

# Open Journaling Space

# Open Journaling Space

# Open Journaling Space

# *Appendix A*

## Quiz Scoring and
## Personality-Profile Inclination(s)

Calculate your score to the flexibility quiz (in the introduction) by counting the total number for each symbol you selected during the quiz:

Total number:  ♣ III   ♥ NHL II   ♦ TFHK IIII   ♠ I

Several scenarios might occur. Some of you might see a clear dominance for one particular profile; however, most people aren't easily put in one box! If you are in the latter group, you probably want to look at the various profiles that you seem to connect with. To visualize the data, draw a bar graph based on your quiz results (see next page).

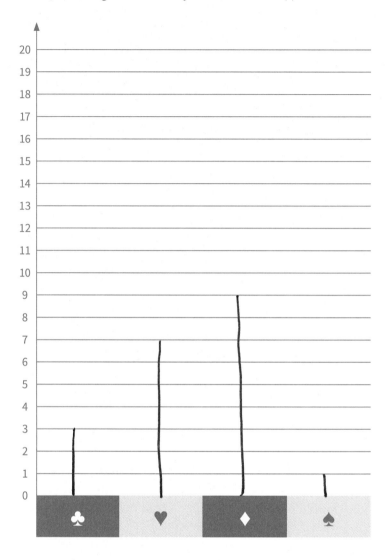

Now take a look at the profile types that emerged as your dominant influences (from your quiz results), and also look at the profiles that only have a minor influence. This quiz doesn't aim to label you but to make you realize your strengths and inclination toward flexibility!

#  Stiff/Preflexible

A lot of people come to yoga thinking, "I can't do this. I'm not flexible enough." This may be your current mindset toward edtech yoga. Your learning-practice muscles may be quite tight, and you might be more inclined to keep your practice the way it is now. You might focus on guiding others around you with your own plan of action; when asked to alter your plan, you might not like it because you want to feel in charge. You tend to be straightforward and take the role of a consultant, telling others what they should do or not do, which may lead them to push through or give up, depending on how your guidance is received. You might not be a big fan of differentiation or personalized learning, thinking that these are simply "buzzwords," as you believe it's hardly ever possible to put these methods into action. Instead, your definition of learning might be centered around behaviorism (practicing by drilling, memorization, or rote learning). With technology, you might prefer to stick with ready-made worksheets, and you closely monitor all students when they're online. And when it comes to encouraging creativity with digital tools, you prefer that everyone follows the specific standards that you set.

You may feel some resistance to the exercises in this book—they are purposely designed to stretch you. But you might find, as others do, that once you start stretching your muscles and gaining flexibility, you will be happy with the results! Therefore, it may require some self-monitoring to ensure that you are stretching yourself appropriately as you read and partic-ipate in the book's exercises.

It's especially important for you to read chapter one and work through all the exercises there. This will help you discover your own vision for *why* you want to improve your learning practice, and it will keep you focused on the results when the journey seems hard. When you read chapter two, remember that it doesn't matter where you are when you start; the important thing is to keep stretching a little further all the time.

We recommend reading *Courageous Edventures: Navigating Obstacles to Discover Classroom Innovation* by Jennie Magiera (2017). This book will guide your first steps into technology integration and innovation as it gently pushes you to overcome your fear of change, allowing you to try new things and to be okay with your failed attempts—necessities to learning and growing. As you read, you will slowly gain confidence in taking new initiatives, relying more and more on collaboration with others, including your colleagues and students.

##  Understretched

Many people start yoga and immediately want to try the difficult poses, but they quickly find out that they need to warm up and try easier postures first; does this reflect how you would approach edtech yoga? If so, you probably like to get out of your comfort zone to take some risks, learn something new, or engage in a collaborative project. However, you might find yourself a bit afraid of trying new and advanced ideas on your own. You are inspired by some educators and look up to them, but you may not see yourself as being able to reach their level. Perhaps you feel a bit underconfident and need to boost your self-esteem.

When it comes to putting your great ideas into practice, do you find that you are left feeling discouraged when they don't work the way you envisioned? For example, you might want to give more agency to your students in their classroom collaborations or be a valuable contributor in a collaborative meeting, but you feel a gap between your aspirations and actions. You would benefit from some guidance in both instances. With technology, you might be too eager to try tools without having tested them, or without planning in depth how the tech will be used in the lesson, and as a result, sometimes it doesn't go the way you thought it would.

Go ahead and jump to chapter four first to learn about different tools that you can incorporate into your classroom practices to engage your students. Look for tools and ideas that may be easier to use and give yourself the chance to test them, warming up to and gaining the skills and stamina you need to go on to the more advanced applications.

We recommend reading *The Innovator's Mindset: Empower Learning, Unleash Talent, and Lead a Culture of Creativity* by George Couros (2015). You are already aware of what innovation is, but you might not understand how it looks in reality—*is* it just a buzzword? This book will allow you to make meaningful connections to this relevant concept, and it will also help you implement new and better ways of teaching, learning, and leading. From vision to action!

#  Flexible

Many people who regularly practice yoga are comfortable using several of familiar poses, but they are often interested in learning something new to stretch themselves further. You may have a similar experience when it comes to edtech yoga—you know the best practices for technology integration in the classroom, and you use them often in your classroom. You feel quite successful in this teaching practice too; while you are at ease and in control, innovating and sharing about your practice, you also think about ways to challenge yourself. However, you might sometimes lack the courage to throw yourself into the unexpected. Sure, you try new things all the time, but what about elevating your craft to the next level? There might be some projects that could transform you and your students and allow you to consider new alternatives. Your support of student agency is strong, though you might wonder how to boost students' voices, choices, and ownership, reducing the number of teacher-led lessons. You are probably fascinated by personalized learning and by growing self-directedness in your students and yourself. You are a learner and an empowerer! In your areas of uncertainty, you just need help going from anxiety to excitement, so you can give it a go.

Go to chapter five to boost your ability to further develop your tinkering mindset. Use these exercises to reconsider what you already know and do, and think outside your comfort zone to challenge yourself. Be increasingly deliberate about your teaching to reach your expected outcomes.

We recommend reading *Show Your Work!: 10 Things Nobody Told You About Getting Discovered* by Austin Kleon (2014). As an agile educator integrating a lot of technology and thriving to continuously improve your practice, you are inspiring and should allow yourself to shine! Watch out for signs of the impostor syndrome: doubting yourself. This book is all about gaining the confidence to show your work even when you feel your work isn't quite ready to be shared. The truth is that nothing is ever perfect, but you will be surprised to see the support you get from others when you share. Everyone benefits!

##  Overstretched

A few yoga practitioners, thinking more is better, stretch farther than they should and injure themselves; this might be the situation you find yourself in with edtech yoga. You might be the type of teacher who strives to always be energetic, dynamic, and excited. As a colleague, you might be the kind who always says, "Yes, and . . . ," and you constantly have a million ideas in mind. Your timetable is full of lessons and meetings, and you volunteer for everything all the time. External recognition is probably important to you too, as you want to have a good reputation. This means competing and showing your work as well.

You likely feel exhausted by this type of overstretching, but we have just the chapter for you! Chapter six discusses the importance of achieving balance by figuring out your most important goals and taking care of yourself.

We recommend reading *Kill the Company: End the Status Quo, Start an Innovation Revolution* by Lisa Bodell (2012). This book encourages you to think about the big picture and reconsider quality over quantity. As you continue your learning journey as a committed educator, you will be able to integrate leadership skills that move you from good to great by operating a change of perspective on your own practice and on the things happening around you. Indeed, there are a lot of practical activities related to change in this book, feeding your thirst for learning and allowing you to focus at the same time!

# *Appendix B*

## Glocal Project Examples

The following table contains glocal (global + local) collaboration projects that connect to the seventh standard in the ISTE Standards for Students—Global Collaborator—with the fourth standard in the ISTE Standards for Educators—Collaborator. The projects range from well known (e.g. Mystery Skype) to smaller initiatives on various topics that are created by teachers around the world. You might be interested in joining some of those existing projects or finding inspiration from them and to start your own glocal initiative.

| Project | Description |
|---|---|
| **Traveling Teddy Bear Project**<br>TravelingTeddyBear.com | Connects young children in classrooms across the globe through the sending and receiving of teddy bears |
| **PenPal Schools**<br>PenPalSchools.com | Connects students with a group of international pen pals. Students learn together and create original projects to share with their local and global peers |
| **Mystery Skype**<br>education.microsoft.com/<br>skype-in-the-classroom/<br>mystery-skype | A global guessing game through Skype that emphasizes the similarities and differences between geographies and cultures |
| **Global Virtual Classroom**<br>VirtualClassroom.org | Empowers, enables, and connects students around the world using a collection of free online activities |

*(continued on next page)*

| Project | Description |
|---|---|
| **Games for Change Student Challenge** gamesforchange.org/studentchallenge | Invites students to make digital games about issues impacting their communities, combining digital storytelling with civic engagement |
| **Cultivate World Literacy** education.microsoft.com/cultivate worldliteracy | Connects students of all ages to join forces and work together to bring about change to an issue that is vital to the world's future |
| **#Decarbonize #Decolonize** Decarbonize.me | Connects and mobilizes youth around the continued impact of colonization and the repercussions on climate change |
| **EdChange Global** EdChangeGlobal.com | Connects teachers and students around the world to share their passion for learning with each other |
| **Five Safe Fingers** mrnamvas.wixsite.com/fivesafefingers | An outstanding example of a glocal project by Nam Ngo Thanh (primary school teacher in Ho Chi Minh City, Vietnam) that aims to raise awareness about child sexual abuse |
| **Global Forest Link** GlobalForestLink.com | An authentic global collaborative-learning project combining environmental science and journalism |

# *Appendix C*

# Digital Citizen Lesson Plans

Created by and for educators, these lesson plans link to the second standard in the ISTE Standards for Students—Digital Citizen. Use them to find all sorts of resources (digital or not) that you can freely reuse or remix to meet your own needs.

| Lesson Plan Theme | Description | Short URL | QR Code |
|---|---|---|---|
| "Cyberbullying & Sexting" (for Grades 10–12) created by Caitlin McLemore using Common Sense Media resources | These lesson plans teach high school students about dangers of online interaction and social media. This includes a critical look at the issues of cyberbullying and sexting with age-appropriate content and discussion topics. | goo.gl/4PnA34 | |
| "Media & Information Literacy" (for Grades 6–10) created by Fanny Passeport and Sunita Malekar | These lesson plans align with two categories of the Approaches to Learning of the International Baccalaureate program and connect to the digital citizen standard in the ISTE Standards for Students; they range from searching online to spotting fake news. | goo.gl/P73b1m | |

# References

Anderson, C. (2016). *TED talks: The official TED guide to public speaking.* New York, NY: Houghton Mifflin Harcourt.

Angelou, M. [OWN]. (2015, January 4). *Dr. Maya Angelou shares one of her greatest lessons / Oprah's Master Class / Oprah Winfrey Network* [Video file]. Retrieved from https://youtu.be/ jvb41H5AjLU

Berg, J., Coller, W., Gormley, T., Johns, G., Jones, S., Kanemoto, C., . . . Suckle, R. (Producers), & Jenkins, P. (Director). (2017). *Wonder woman* [Motion picture]. United States: Warner Bros. Pictures.

Bodell, L. (2012). *Kill the company: End the status quo, start an innovation revolution.* Brookline, MA: Bibliomotion.

Bronfenbrenner, U. (1979). *The ecology of human development: Experiments by nature and design.* Cambridge, MA: Harvard University Press.

Brookfield, S. D. (2017). *Becoming a critically reflective teacher.* San Francisco, CA: Jossey-Bass.

Brown, B. (2012). *Daring greatly: How the courage to be vulnerable transforms the way we live, love, parent, and lead.* New York, NY: Random House.

Brown, B. (2015). *Rising strong: How the ability to rest transforms the way we live, love, parent, and lead.* New York, NY: Random House.

Christakis, N. & Fowler, J. (2009). *Connected: The surprising power of our social networks and how they shape our lives.* New York, NY: Little, Brown and Company.

Clark, C. M. & Peterson, P. L. (1986). Teachers' thought processes. In M. C. Wittrock (Ed.), *Handbook of research on teaching* (pp. 255–296). New York, NY: Macmillan.

Collins, A. & Halverson, R. (2009). *Rethinking education in the age of technology: The digital revolution and schooling in america.* New York, NY: Teachers College Press.

Collins, A. & Halverson, R. (2010). The second educational revolution: Rethinking education in the age of technology. *Journal of Computer Assisted Learning, 26,* 18–27. doi:10.1111/j.1365-2729.2009.00339.x

Collins, J. C. (2001). *Good to great: Why some companies make the leap . . . and others don't.* New York, NY: HarperCollins.

Cordy, M. [ISTE]. (2016, December 20). *ISTE 2016 keynote speaker Michelle Cordy / Connect with your PLN to empower & engage students* [Video file]. Retrieved from https://youtu.be/ wL0XZsxYeKw

Costa, A. L. & Garmston, R. J. (with Hayes, C. & Ellison, J.). (2016). *Cognitive coaching: Developing self-directed leaders and learners.* (3rd ed.). Lanham, MD: Rowman & Littlefield.

Costa, A. L. & Kallick, B. (Eds.). (1995). Systems thinking: Interactive assessment in holonomous organizations. In Costa, A. L. & Kallick, B. (Eds.). *Assessment in the learning organization: Shifting the paradigm.* Association for Supervision and Curriculum Development. Retrieved from http://www.ascd.org/publications/books/195188/chapters/Systems-Thinking@-Interactive-Assessment-in-Holonomous-Organizations.aspx

Couros, G. (2015). *The innovator's mindset: Empower learning, unleash talent, and lead a culture of creativity.* San Diego, CA: Dave Burgess Consulting.

Covey, S. (1989). *The 7 habits of highly effective people: Powerful lessons in personal change.* New York, NY: Free Press.

Cuddy, A. J. (2015). *Presence: Bringing your boldest self to your biggest challenges.* New York, NY: Back Bay Books.

Cuddy, A. J. [QuickTalks]. (2016, July 8). *How to be yourself in conversation / Amy Cuddy (summary)* [Video file]. Retrieved from https://youtu.be/YcGd5eBwQU4

Dhingra, R. [TEDx Talks]. (2012, June 15). *Can technology change education? Yes!: Raj Dhingra at TEDxBend* [Video file]. Retrieved from https://youtu.be/l0s_M6xKxNc

Drago-Severson, E. & Blum-DeStefano, J. (2016). *Tell me so I can hear you: A developmental approach to feedback for educators.* Cambridge, MA: Harvard Education Press.

Duckworth, A. [TED Talks Education]. (2013, April). *Grit: The power of passion and perseverance* [Video file]. Retrieved from https://www.ted.com/talks/ angela_lee_duckworth_grit_the_power_of_passion_and_perseverance/ transcript?nolanguage=sp

Duckworth, S. (2016). *Sketchnotes for educators.* Irvine, CA: EdTechTeam Press.

Durant, W. (1961). *The story of philosophy: The lives and opinions of the world's greatest philosophers.* New York, NY: Simon & Schuster.

Dweck, C. S. (2006). *Mindset: The new psychology of success.* New York, NY: Ballantine Books.

Ertmer, P. A. & Newby, T. J. (1993). Behaviorism, cognitivism, constructivism: Comparing critical features from an instructional design perspective. *Performance Improvement Quarterly, 6*(4), 50–72. doi:10.1111/j.1937-8327.1993.tb00605.x

Favre, D. (2015). *Cessons de démotiver les élèves—2e éd.: 19 clés pour favoriser l'apprentissage.* Dunod.

Foege, A. (2013). *The tinkerers: The amateurs, DIYers, and inventors who make America great.* New York, NY: Basic Books.

Garcia, H. & Miralles, F. (2016). *Ikigai: The Japanese secret to a long and happy life.* New York, NY: Penguin Books.

Garmston, R. J. & Von Frank, V. (2012). *Unlocking group potential to improve schools.* Thousand Oaks, CA: Corwin Press.

Garmston, R. J. & Wellman, B. M. (2016). *The adaptive school: A sourcebook for developing collaborative groups.* (3rd ed.). Lanham, MD: Rowman & Littlefield.

Gattegno, C. (1977). On mistakes. *Educational Solutions Worldwide Newsletter, 6*(2–3). Retrieved from http://subtle-ed.site/wp-content/uploads/2015/11/1104_2_3-On-Mistakes-December-1976-February-1977.pdf

Gattegno, C. (1987a). *The science of education: Part I: Theoretical considerations.* New York, NY: Educational Solutions Worldwide.

Gattegno, C. (1987b). *What we owe children: The subordination of teaching.* New York, NY: Educational Solutions Worldwide.

Ginopolis, M. (2011, February 28). *Digitaleading: Part II* [Blog post]. Retrieved from http:// bigthink.com/articles/digitaleading-part-ii

International Society for Technology in Education. (2016). ISTE Standards for Students. Retrieved from iste.org/standards/for-students

International Society for Technology in Education. (2017). ISTE Standards for Educators. Retrieved from iste.org/standards/for-educators

Kelley, T. & Kelley, D. (2013). *Creative confidence: Unleashing the creative potential within us all.* New York, NY: Crown Business.

Kleon, A. (2014). *Show your work!: 10 things nobody told you about getting discovered.* New York, NY: Workman.

Knight, J. (2011). *Unmistakable impact: A partnership approach for dramatically improving instruction.* Thousand Oaks, CA: Corwin Press.

Koyenikan, I. (2016) *Wealth for All: Living a Life of Success at the Edge of Your Ability.* Fuquay-Varina, NC: Grandeur Touch, LLC.

Lin, D. (Producer) Lord, P., & Miller, C. (Directors). (2014). *The LEGO movie* [DVD]. United States: Warner Home Video.

Lucas, G. (Producer), & Kershner, I. (Director). (1980). *Star Wars: Episode V—The empire strikes back* [Motion picture]. United States: Lucasfilm.

Magiera, J. (2017). *Courageous adventures: Navigating obstacles to discover classroom innovation.* Thousand Oaks, CA: Corwin Press.

Martin, T. [Tara Martin]. (2017, August 31). *#BookSnaps Snapchat for annotation ISTE 2017— R.E.A.L. Talk w/Tara M. Martin episode 25* [Video file]. Retrieved from https://youtu.be/_yfRNxNo1Ss

Martinez, S. L. & Stager, G. (2013). *Invent to learn: Making, tinkering, and engineering in the classroom.* Torrance, CA: Constructing Modern Knowledge Press.

Marzano, R. J. & Kendall, J. S. (2007). *The new taxonomy of educational objectives.* (2nd ed.). Thousand Oaks, CA: Corwin Press.

Mehta, N. [TEDx Talks]. (2012, February 26). *TEDxBerkeley—Nipun Mehta—Designing for generosity* [Video file]. Retrieved from https://youtu.be/kpyc84kamhw

Miller, M. [Ditch That Textbook]. (2016, February 1). *Innovating in the classroom* [Video file]. Retrieved from https://youtu.be/NL9lAYzMQ-M

Neal, J. W. & Neal, Z. P. (2013). Nested or networked? Future directions for ecological systems theory. *Social Development, 22,* 722–737. doi:10.1111/sode.12018

Neff, K. (2018). *Exercise 3: Exploring self-compassion through writing* [Website]. Retrieved from http://self-compassion.org/exercise-3-exploring-self-compassion-writing

Passeport, F. (2017). Developing "glocal" mindsets in the primary years. *Future Forwards, 7,* 19–28. Retrieved from http://www.asbfutureforwards-digital.com/asbfutureforwards/vol7?pg=21#pg21

Perkins, D. (1998). What is understanding? In Wiske, M. S. (Ed.), *Teaching for understanding: Linking research with practice* (pp. 39–57). San Francisco, CA: Jossey-Bass.

Pink, D. H. (2010). *Drive: The surprising truth about what motivates us.* New York, NY: Riverhead Books.

Pink, D. H. (2018). *When: The science of timing.* New York, NY: Riverhead Books.

Rath, T. (2007). *Strengthsfinder 2.0: Discover your CliftonStrengths.* New York, NY: Gallup.

Ritchhart, R., Church, M., & Morrison, K. (2011). *Making thinking visible: How to promote engagement, understanding, and independence for all learners.* San Francisco, CA: Jossey-Bass.

Roth, W. (2015). Becoming aware: Towards a post-constructivist theory of learning. *Learning: Research and Practice, 1,* 38–50. doi:10.1080/23735082.2015.994256

Saltzberg, B. (2010). *Beautiful oops!* New York, NY: Workman.

Sandberg, S. (2013). *Lean In: Women, work, and the will to lead.* New York, NY: Alfred A. Knopf.

Scharmer, C. O. (2009). *Theory U: Leading from the future as it emerges.* San Francisco, CA: Berrett-Koehler.

Scharmer, C. O. (2018). *The essentials of Theory U: Core principles and applications.* Oakland, CA: Berrett-Koehler.

Shavelson, R. J. (1973). What is the basic teaching skill? *Journal of Teacher Education, 24,* 144–151. doi:10.1177/002248717302400213

Sinek, S. (2011). *Start with why: how great leaders inspire everyone to take action.* New York, NY: The Penguin Group.

Stone, D. & Heen, S. (2014). *Thanks for the feedback: The science and art of receiving feedback well (even when it is off base, unfair, poorly delivered, and frankly, you're not in the mood).* New York, NY: Penguin Group.

Suzuki, S. (2011). *Zen mind, beginner's mind: Informal talks on Zen meditation and practice.* Boston, MA: Shambala.

Thoreau, H. D. (1995). *Walden, or, life in the woods.* Mineola, NY: Dover Publications.

Tinker. (n.d.). In *Merriam-Webster's online dictionary.* Retrieved from https://www.merriam-webster.com/dictionary/tinkering

UX Mastery. (n.d.). *Reverse it* [Website]. Retrieved from https://www.designgames.com.au/reverse_it

Winn, M. (2014, May 14). *What is your ikigai?* [Blog]. Retrieved from http://theviewinside.me/what-is-your-ikigai

Wood Brooks, A. & John, K. L. (2018, May–June). The surprising power of questions. *Harvard Business Review.* Retrieved from https://hbr.org/2018/05/the-surprising-power-of-questions

Yamada, K. (2014). *What do you do with an idea?* Seattle, WA: Compendium.

Young, R. (2011). *L'anglais avec l'approche Silent Way.* Paris, France: Eyrolles.

Young, R. & Messum, P. (2011). *How we learn and how we should be taught: An introduction to the work of Caleb Gattegno (Vol. 1).* London, England: Duo Flumina.

# Index